A Man
Seen Afar

by

WELLESLEY TUDOR POLE

and

ROSAMOND LEHMANN

With a foreword by

SIR GEORGE TREVELYAN, BT. M.A.

NEVILLE SPEARMAN

Other Works by W. Tudor Pole:

The Silent Road

Writing on the Ground

Private Dowding

My Dear Alexias
(Letters to Rosamond Lehmann)

New Edition June 1983

ISBN 85435 085 3

Printed in Great Britain by Redwood Burn Ltd, Trowbridge, Wiltshire for the publishers, Neville Spearman Ltd, Priory Gate, Friars Street, Sudbury, Suffolk.

Contents

Foreword

by Sir George Trevelyan, Bt, M.A.

IN THIS book W. Tudor Pole submits what purport to be memories of the life and time of Jesus. This will be received by some with deep interest, by others with incredulity. If the claim is valid the publication of these writings at this time could be most significant.

The manner of appearance of these 'memories' is most interesting and is highly relevant to the state of consciousness of modern man. Tudor Pole in his introduction tells us that these recollections came into his mind with the clarity of normal memory, 'as if he had been there', and he submits this record, in all humility, as a genuine glimpse into the past.

To him these recollections are emphatically not the product of imagination: that word has been debased into meaning the weaving of fantasies. In its true sense it implies an entry by pictorial thinking into a higher 'frequency', a world of reality and being, beyond the limitations of the five senses. This is the first step in research and exploration into the spiritual realms which interpenetrate our physical world of life and being.

When these 'recollections' came they conveyed to Tudor Pole the conviction that they were true and real. He felt that the unexpected suddenness of their coming into his mind was an indication that they came for a purpose and should therefore be shared with others. In doing so he takes the risk of being regarded as a mere dreamer. It is important therefore to attempt some bridge to an understanding of these writings.

These 'memories' are an example of something developing today in human thinking. In our age we are getting a new understanding of the truth that the spiritual realms absolutely interpenetrate the physical. Indeed the world of material forms is seen as an image or reflection of the spiritual which creates it. The realms of spirit are not far distant but lie within the sense world and are to be grasped there by our intuitive thinking.

The 'new understanding' is but the re-appearance of the Ancient Wisdom which was taught in the mystery temples to the candidates for initiation. He who revealed the secret teachings lost his life. The esoteric knowledge was passed down through the generations, appearing in each age in a different form, sometimes acceptable and often misunderstood. It is hidden in the allegory of mythology and great drama, and can be re-interpreted through the psychological understanding of our age. With the development of intellectual consciousness it becomes possible for this Ancient Wisdom to be published in books and given in open lectures in a form acceptable to the modern mind.

We have reached a stage in our largely materialistic

culture when very many people are hungry for understanding of the reality of the spiritual worlds. These realms have always existed, but we are cut off from them so long as we rely only on the five outward senses for our knowledge. Now we find that a purely mechanistic explanation of the universe is wholly inadequate. Even matter is not rightly explained unless we can see it as the outcome of divine thought and creative imagination. It is of immense importance to consider all clues concerning the true nature of man and life. The contents of this book may well give such a clue.

'Memory' as understood here implies the postulate of previous earth lives. In the 'sensitive', memory of earlier lives on earth can rise to consciousness in the form of pictures. Furthermore it is possible, in the consciousness which is lifted beyond the five senses, to experience what lived in another soul. A kind of telepathy is possible so that one person may 'remember' what another experienced long ago.

This is illumined by the important concept of what are sometimes called the Akashic Records. 'Akasha' is the name given by Ancient Wisdom to what is conceived as a spiritual substance of great subtlety surrounding the material earth like a sheath into which all impulses of thought, emotion and will are imprinted or recorded. In a sense, trivial though the comparison is, it may be thought of as a great etheric tape recorder. Those who are sufficiently advanced in consciousness are able to 'read' this record and actually listen, within their own intuitive thinking, to the experiences of souls in past history. This is a primary source for spiritual research.

We must grasp the fact that our thoughts and feelings are

9

in a real sense alive. When we send them forth we have
created something which does not, as we too easily imagine,
disappear, but has in it the nature of a being which enters a
timeless realm, may be read by initiate minds, and which we
shall meet again when released from the limitations of the
body. If this concept could be understood, people today
would be less free with their criticism, their cynicism and
the cruelty of their thinking. We can indeed add a jet of
darkness or of light to the timeless realms each time we
send out a thought or express an emotion.

These 'memories' of this author appear to be readings of
the Akashic Record. It is not of primary significance whether
he is remembering his personal experiences or 'reading'
those of other souls with whom he was connected in a past
time. What matters for us is the possibility that we are here
given a direct picture of the life of our Lord.

The faculties of inner perception are present in every one
of us with a greater or lesser degree of development and
sensitivity. It may well be that others can begin to throw
light on this period of history through their own 'recollections'. It would seem that, although deception is very easy,
the real remembrances carry a very special conviction of their
truth. Such a flood of new knowledge and spiritual understanding is now entering our thinking that this volume
may be only one of many which will be given to the world
from higher sources.

Its publication is particularly relevant at this time when
much new light is being thrown on the life of Jesus by the
interpretation of the Dead Sea Scrolls and from other
sources. Many who are interested in spiritual matters are
filled with the conviction that in some ways there is now a

heightening of spiritual tension and an entry of spiritual power into our world which may have the nature of a 'Second Coming'. A new light is flooding into human consciousness and the Christ impulse may be coming afresh into our lives. We may expect revelation of new truths; and perhaps these recollections are really sent to help us to understand the great changes taking place, and the immense hope which can fill our hearts and inspire our thoughts and actions.

Introduction

by Rosamond Lehmann

THE MAJOR portion of this volume is the fruit of my collaboration with Wellesley Tudor Pole, 'Guide, Philosopher and Friend' to how many others besides myself! Since he prefers that as little as possible of his personal history should be discussed (he is, he says, 'an ordinary man'), I will confine myself to an outline of the main achievements of his long and distinguished career.

He has married and brought up a family, engaged in industry and other mundane affairs, travelled widely in the Middle East, 'risked his life when the risk served a worth while purpose', and undertaken archaeological research in various parts of the world. He is a lifelong student of healing as applied to man, animals and trees. In 1959 he acquired the long-neglected Chalice Well property at Glastonbury and founded the Trust of that name. He is also a Governor of the Glaston Tor preparatory School for boys; and the author of two works, remarkable, indeed unique, in their particular field: *Private Dowding* and *The*

Silent Road*; as well as of other publications. He was also the founder, in 1940, of the Big Ben Silent Minute.

I will add, I hope with his permission, that not unlike William Blake, he combines simplicity, warmth of nature and astringent humour with intellectual vigour; that his mysticism, like Blake's, is practical and joyous. He too 'looks back into the Regions of Reminiscence and beholds our ancient days'; but always in order to look forward and outward; not to dwell shuttered and enclosed therein.

From henceforth he will be referred to, again with his permission, by his initials, w.t.p.

The character of the texts that follow is largely explained by Sir George Trevelyan in his admirable Foreword. All I can usefully add is a more personal light on the sequence of events that led to my assuming the editorial and other labours connected with the material entrusted to me by w.t.p.

It was in the winter of 1962/63 that our paths first crossed. At that time I was still struggling to recover from a bereavement so shattering that the blow had seemed mortal: I mean, the death, far away from me, in Java, in her twenty-third year and the second year of her marriage, of my only daughter Sally. My object in speaking of her here is to make it clear that Midsummer Eve, 1958—the day she left the earth—was the day of the beginning of a total *metanoia* in my way of living, thinking and experiencing. That chronicle is being written: this is not the place to enlarge upon it further. Between 1958 and 1962 I had made certain discoveries on my own account; I had also learned much from people further advanced than I in spiritual under-

*Published by Neville Spearman—1960.

standing; but I was still far from any true, or at least firmly-based measure of 'recovery' or of enlightenment. 'When the pupil is ready . . .' perhaps! In any case I owe w.t.p. an immeasurable debt of gratitude for the (by me) unlooked-for interest he took in my welfare, and for the metaphysical grounding which I received from him.

It seems to me best to incorporate here w.t.p.'s own version of our first encounter and its consequences. He writes:

'It was at Christmastide 1958 that recollections of certain events immediately preceding the Last Supper became sufficiently tangible in my mind to set down on paper.

'I had recently returned from a visit to Chalice Well, Glastonbury, and it was therefore natural that my thoughts should be filled with events connected with the times of Jesus, and Avalon as the traditional cradle of the Christian faith in Britain. I hesitated for some months before deciding to publish this very fragmentary reminiscence in the hope that further "glimpses" of a similar kind would follow. In this I was disappointed; and so in June 1959 I arranged for *The Upper Room** to be published in booklet form, followed by a short Commentary.

'During the next few years, and usually at unexpected moments, I found myself trying to bring into perspective a panorama of incidents and events which seemed to be unrolling within the recesses of my mind. Instinctively I connected these shadowy experiences with my memory of the "Upper Room"; but the pictures were far too misty and kaleidoscopic for identification.

The Upper Room, with a commentary by W. Tudor Pole, published by The Chalice Well Trust, Glastonbury, Somerset.

'In the Autumn of 1962, when sitting in the Chalice Well Orchard, wondering how to secure clarity of vision, this intimation flashed on me: "Cease worrying—when the right time, place, and conditions coincide, your vision and your memory will come into correct focus".

'This intimation was conveyed with so much authority that perplexities vanished, and I went my way relieved. Subsequently and from time to time I found myself wondering if the promise contained in the intimation would be fulfilled; and if so, when, where and under what particular conditions.

'In some strange way I felt within me the capacity to strike sparks; but that if these sparks were destined to flower into more than a fleeting illumination, an "anvil" outside myself and of a special kind was needed: one provided by the presence in my life of a companion, an understanding comrade, capable of nurturing into an enduring flame whatever sparks were struck.

'During the winter of 1962-63 a mutual friend introduced me to Madame Simone Saint-Clair, the well-known French patriot and writer; and it was through this gracious and talented lady that, in due course, a book of mine was translated and published in Paris under the title *La Route du Graal*. Early in 1963 I received several letters from Madame Saint-Clair urging me to call upon a great friend of hers, living in London, saying that she felt that this contact would prove important and mutually beneficial. It was then that I received the impression that time, place and conditions were about to wheel into line, and that perhaps the "anvil" I had subconsciously been seeking was near at hand. This proved to be the case, for shortly afterwards

R.L. came into my life and I into hers.

'When I look back, I realize that there is nothing strange in the fact that one of the first subjects we discussed was the contents of *The Upper Room* and the way in which this little book had come into being.

'As our friendship ripened, I began to realize that the stage was in truth being set for the long-awaited fulfilment of the promise made to me at Glastonbury in the Autumn of 1962. All things began to work harmoniously together, and co-operation between R.L. and W.T.P. became close and continuous.

'For a period covering little more than a month in the summer of 1963, at irregular intervals, usually late at night in my Sussex home, many of the "glimpses" of Jesus' boyhood and youth recorded later in this book were visualised, "captured" and set down in writing.'

I (R.L.) must add that I never knew until quite recently, when I received a copy of the account just quoted, why it was that W.T.P. selected me for a task so tremendous in its potential implications. Late in the summer of 1963 it was suggested to me that I should, if I would, edit, arrange, comment upon and generally prepare for publication the material which had been confided to me. I did not—still do not—consider myself fitted for the work. Nothing qualified me for it in my own opinion; but since no one less unfitted seemed available, and since the invitation came from W.T.P., I felt bound to accept it; and did so with hesitation and trepidation; above all with a genuine sense of being privileged far beyond my deserts.

W.T.P., who sometimes chooses to be literal-minded, replied, when I mentioned 'holy dread', that there was no such thing; that dread and holiness are concepts mutually and altogether incompatible. Nevertheless, so far as I am concerned, this phrase of Coleridge's hits the mark, as poets' phrases do. With something approaching holy dread I embarked upon, continued, and completed my part in our collaboration.

Credo

by W.T.P.

IT HAS BEEN suggested that I should give some details about my own religious outlook. This I am quite ready to do.

I was christened and confirmed into the Church of England, the outlook of my parents in those days being what used to be known as 'broad Church'. My religious training was based mainly on that form of Public School Christianity which includes the thesis that the Bible (King James' Authorised English version) is the established Word of God in every particular and therefore contains the whole Truth and nothing but the Truth. I was a thoughtful lad, and it was not long before I began to doubt very seriously the dogmatic assertion which has just been quoted. As an instance, there are certain passages in the early Books of the Old Testament which seemed to my youthful mind to border on the obscene. When on one occasion I asked the School Chaplain to explain the religious significance of such passages, he instructed me to confine my attention to the contents of the New Testament alone. In this connection I remember an occasion in my fifteenth year when I noted and wrote down a list of contradictions concerning the life and teaching of Jesus, as given in the four Gospels and in the Acts of the Apostles. This I submitted to my Form Master when called upon to write an essay on the Ten Commandments.

Needless to say I received the lowest marks in the class for this outrageous example of precocity; but no explanation was forthcoming to allay my doubts and misgivings.

It was soon after this that I gave up asking questions and began to work out a philosophy of my own, much of which has stood the test of time.

My religious outlook, following a long life of reflection and experience, could now be summed up, by no means comprehensively, as follows:

I believe in a First Cause, a supreme Creator of all the Universes, the Origin of Life itself, a Mind both Eternal and Omnipotent, Father of Infinite Love, Wisdom and Integrity.

I believe that in ways far beyond human comprehension this First Cause has brought into being the solar systems, the planets and the stars, together with countless other realms of life and being stretching forth into the infinitude of Eternity.

I believe that Truth in its absolute sense lies beyond our human ken at present, but that Life in every form and manifestation is evolving toward an ultimate goal which we call Perfection. And that this mysterious process has continued and will continue for so many millions of 'light' years as to be far beyond the range of human speculation.

In so far as our own planet is concerned, I believe that it

is the most external of seven realms of consciousness, corresponding in a certain way to the seven Kingdoms of Nature that are known to us. And that these seven realms form a unit in the sense that Life and Intelligence, however clothed or embodied within them, progress (and at times retrogress) as a whole toward a far-off goal of infinite but unknown importance. I believe that this process is directed by a Being who might be called the Ruler of the Planet; One who is under the control of the Supreme Governor of the solar system to which we belong; He Himself being subject to the First Cause.

I believe that at what may seem to us to be irregular intervals in human time, Saviours and Messengers from cosmic realms descend into our midst to found and inspire what for our level of consciousness appear to be new religions, philosophies and ethical systems of belief and conduct.

Of these great Messengers I believe that Jesus, whilst overshadowed by the Being we call the Christ, brought down into human consciousness a larger measure of inspiration and truth than any of his predecessors.

I believe that the time is near when we may expect another of these cosmic visitations, bringing with it what will result in an extended and enlarged understanding of Truth, in its eternal sense; thereby bringing us one step nearer to the comprehension of the enigma of existence and its purpose.

I believe that the Supreme Creator can be worshipped with equal value in temple, church, synagogue, mosque or in the open air; or within the inner sanctuary of our own being.

Using conventional language, I believe in the Communion of Saints, the existence of Angels and Archangels, and the Power of Spirit as an all-pervading presence.

I believe that a God (in embryo) exists within every individualised manifestation of Life, and that Life itself is eternal and indestructible; that 'death' as meaning permanent extinction has no place in the Universe and never has and never will. Life can change its form but never die.

I believe in our return to this earth on more than one occasion as an integral part of the evolutionary process. It is only here that we can receive certain training and experience which would be unavailable to us on other levels of consciousness.

I believe that what we call Evil is temporary illusion operating within the human mind, a form of energy which for the time being is misdirected and out of control, but which is capable of re-direction into harmonious channels, when it ceases to be 'Evil'.

I believe in the eternal existence of absolute Love and Wisdom; and that as children of the One Creator we can each draw our inspiration and our guidance from them according to our needs and in direct relation to our deserts.

I believe in the ultimate brotherhood, with unity of purpose, between all manifestations of life and intelligence not only on our own planet but throughout the countless universes that God has created and energised with Life.

The Upper Room

A description of the house in Jerusalem where the Last Supper was held.

IT WAS NOT a large house, but built solidly of stone, and there were two doors only. This house was just within the city's limits in a narrow cobbled street and standing in its own ground. Behind the house there was a small walled enclosure. This contained the household well and a fig tree against the wall. There was also a bushy thorn tree growing in a corner and this was in early bud. There were no figs visible on the tree but some young green leaves were showing. The well appeared to be half dry, with very little water visible in its depths. Leaning against the house in this courtyard was a stone shelter which contained a carpenter's bench, chopped wood, also a large earthenware jar of wine and a flagon of olive oil. At the side of the house a wooden annexe had been built, a small stable, which was half filled with straw and housed a donkey who had just come in from work at the time of our visit. The front door of this modest dwelling was flush with the street. On entering, one found oneself in a room of some size, with a large hearth, stone slabbed. A deep alcove for cooking adjoined the living room. On the other side were two smaller rooms, used for sleeping quarters.

When we arrived, which was towards eventide, two small children were asleep in one of these rooms. The other was empty. The beds consisted of straw mattresses raised from the floors on wooden trestles. No carpets were on the floors, but these were partly covered by flaxen or fibrous mats into which coloured designs had been woven. The furnishing was simple, but the whole house was scrupulously clean and well kept. The walls were bare except for two camel-hair rugs. These were hooded at one end and were evidently for use as cloaks in cold weather.

You may ask why the contents of this particular house, humble dwelling as it is, should be described in so much detail. It happens to be a very important house indeed. A man bearing a pitcher of water had led us to the front door. He went on but we delayed our entry for a while. He was a kinsman of the good man to whom this house belonged. The message which had followed on his heels made much stir, and preparations were put in hand at once to get ready an upper room and to lay a meal for about a dozen people. Two of these had arrived with the water carrier.

On going upstairs we found that apart from one large room, almost under the eaves and in appearance not unlike an extensive garret, this upper floor only contained a small bedroom divided from the large room by a short passage. This smaller room was being converted into an annexe for the service of the meal in course of preparation downstairs.

The warm smell of cooking reached us from below. A long narrow table on trestles almost filled the guest chamber, and around it were being placed hand-made stools with short legs, and these appeared to be made of cedar or pear wood. The table itself had evidently been fashioned by a master craftsman, and was in process of being oiled and polished. It was made of olive wood. There was no glass in the windows, which were covered with transparent gauze that let the light and air through but prevented the entry of mosquitoes and other insects. The day had been sultry and the atmosphere was close, most unusual for so early in the year. Behind the door a smaller table had been brought up from the living room. On it was laid a platter containing dried fish, a flask of olive oil and a basket filled with lettuce and other salad greens and bitter herbs. A plate made of baked clay filled with broken pieces of unleavened bread was already in place, also a bowl of fruit: lemons, dried figs, dates and nuts. Towards the centre of the table, but on the floor beside it, stood an earthenware jar containing wine. A stone pitcher of water kept it company. No silver or china cups or metal mugs or plates were to be seen, but there were hand-made drinking vessels on the table. What seemed unusual was the presence of a large and fairly deep wooden bowl placed at the centre of the table, a bowl (now empty) which would be capable of holding a considerable quantity of wine or other liquid. It was the custom in some Jewish households, on ceremonial occasions, to fill such bowls with wine. This perhaps explained the presence of the flagon of wine on the floor, the contents of which could be poured into the table bowl, as the need arose. One other detail: near the stool on which the principal guest would be seated had been placed a shallow saucer-like 'cup' made of glass, multi-coloured yet silvery hued and of fine semi-transparent design. The giver of the feast or the principal guest would dip this 'cup' into the large bowl standing in the centre of the table, and after blessing it would pass it round to all present so that they might drink from it sacramentally one by one. I noticed three terracotta 'lamps' on the table: a large one near the centre and a smaller one at either end. These lamps were closed except for a small aperture in the spout where unlighted wicks were floating in the oil. In shape they were not unlike the modern teapot and probably contained enough oil to burn for several hours. In one of the corners of the room under the eaves an object was visible that looked like a kind of lantern, otherwise there appeared to be no further means for lighting the room when darkness descended. It seemed likely that this chamber was not in general use, but only opened up at the time of Passover and for similar ceremonial purposes.

As we left this upper room to go downstairs, a shaft of light from the setting sun lit it up and gave a certain splendour to the scene. When we met the good man of the house to say goodbye he told us that he was by trade a mason and also a wood carver. Evidently he was proud of the special office which he said he held, namely, Convenor of the Guild of Master Masons and Carpenters. I asked him about the 'cup' which has already been described. He told us that it was held in much reverence, and he believed that it had been made by a craftsman of Antioch, near which city could be found, in the desert, a particular 'vein' of white silica suitable for glass-making. Such hand-made glassware was a feature of the industry of Antioch, he said. It was still being sold and at modest prices through Asia Minor, Syria and Palestine and was even exported to Egypt, Italy and elsewhere in the Roman Empire.

In bidding us farewell he told us he understood that the approaching feast was to be a great occasion, and that he and his good wife felt both honoured and humbled to think that their house had been chosen for the purpose, although it was a mystery to them because the guests to be expected were strangers, so far as he then knew. Among them, he had been told, would be a very holy man, perhaps a 'Master'; and he asked us to hold himself and all his household in our thoughts and prayers.

On leaving the house my companion and I stood silent for a while. Then he gave me his blessing and went his way, turning down a side-lane, crossing the brook and proceeding towards the lower slopes of the Mount of Olives.

I walked up the street in the opposite direction until I reached a vantage point from where the house we had just left was still in view. As I stood there, watching, the stars came out and an evening mist arose from the valley below. Dimly from afar I witnessed the arrival of the Master and his ten companions, and saw them entering the house I had so recently and so reluctantly left behind me. It was then that I became aware of a deep but brilliant glow spreading from the house in all directions and illuminating the darkness of the night. Later still I heard the sound of singing. Then I went my way to my home on the other side of the city, filled with a feeling of impending tragedy, and yet with an underlying sense of joy and thanksgiving which has remained with me ever since.

To this narrative, w.t.p. appends the following note:

26

There is no historical evidence available to confirm the contents of the above narrative. It is however based on an experience which the writer believes, in substance, to represent the facts.

R.L.: A first reading of *The Upper Room* caused me to experience that kind of shock, as of inner recognition, that stills the attention without conscious effort; and on a level that seems to make questions of 'evidence' or 'proof' irrelevant. Some 'touchstone' quality, or mixture of qualities, inherent in this mysterious narrative—its simplicity, its matter-of-fact care for detail, its crystalline transparency, its tone of authority combined with self-effacement— moved and impressed me profoundly. Many besides myself have been similarly moved by it; and every subsequent reading has consolidated my primary conviction that the author had been 'shown', accurately, in detail, the room in which the Last Supper was held.

Some months later this supplementary glimpse was given me, unsought, in a letter.

W.T.P.: I shall never forget with what vigour and respectful solicitation the good man tried to persuade Jesus to remain in his house for the night. He was horrified to hear of Jesus going out into the darkness—especially when civil disturbance was in the air—with the intention of spending the remainder of the night out of doors. He offered his donkey for Jesus to ride, and the services of his own close kinsman as a protection. But Jesus seemed as if in a state of suspended animation, and he replied not, but led the disciples out into the garden and the hill slopes beyond. (I have often tarried there in my present life, both physically and otherwise.)

Later still I was given the opportunity to question w.t.p. on certain points in the Upper Room narrative that continued to perplex me. Here are my questions, and the answers (not always consecutively received) which he has permitted me to publish.

r.l.: Is the 'I' of the narrative yourself?

w.t.p.: The 'I' of the narrative was the individual whose mind I was reading . . . or if you like riding, at the time when these events took place. He was a citizen of standing, half Syrian, half Greek, who must have been brought into the tapestry because the 'companion' needed to have with him a being in full possession of his vitality and his magnetic body to help in the preparation of the Room Upstairs.

By the way, very few of the so-called Jesus sites now extant are geographically correct. For instance the house (long long ago destroyed) containing the Upper Room was not at the summit of Mount Zion, where a tumbledown church still stands; but a good way down, on its eastern slope.

r.l.: Who was the 'companion'?

w.t.p.: The companion was angelic—not a denizen of earth in an ordinary physical body. The atmosphere into which Jesus was about to enter on this immensely important occasion had to be protectively prepared against the Forces of Negation. Such preparations were always made in advance for Jesus throughout his life on earth.

r.l.: Who was the man bearing a pitcher of water?

w.t.p.: As the narrative tells you, he was a kinsman of the master of the house. I've forgotten his name. He arrived with Peter and John. 'My companion and I' (not recorded in the Gospels) followed. Peter and John remained in the house to supervise the making ready of the Passover. (Hence, of course the reference, in the last paragraph, to the arrival of the Master and only ten companions.)

R.L.: I questioned W.T.P. about the multi-coloured 'cup' or bowl of glass so vividly described. It would seem, from what he told me, to have a tangled history, both factual and esoteric. This vessel, or its exact replica, still exists; and is known to have been the subject of numerous conflicting opinions and conjectures. One day perhaps the truth about it will be brought to light; but apparently the time is not yet ripe. Meanwhile it is in safe keeping.

What follows now is W.T.P.'s considered reply to various questions of mine with regard to the faculty of memory. It can be usefully studied as a preface to the 'glimpses' of the life and times of Jesus which were given to me during the summer and autumn of 1963; mostly in letters; occasionally in the course of conversations. These latter I have continued to record in dialogue form, from full notes taken at the time; and the former have been extracted, with W.T.P.'s permission and approval, from our voluminous private correspondence. My hope is that one day further material derived from the same source, equally remarkable but less relevant to W.T.P.'s present purpose, may be considered (by him) publishable.

Meanwhile, as regards what follows, I have here and there (again with permission) substituted a few sentences and phrases of my own for his; also knit up certain broken sequences into an ordered narrative; but never, I need hardly say, enlarged upon, suppressed or in any way tampered with the essence of the original material entrusted to me.

The decision to include certain perhaps extraneous Notes and Comments (such as that on Reincarnation) within the framework of this book was mine.

W.T.P.: The Mind of Man is the most wonderful instrument in his possession. Without it his life would be a living death.

The three main functions of mind are the capacity to think (to reason); the power to feel (to love); and the ability to recollect (to memorise).

When I think I know that I exist and am alive.

When I feel I know that love exists and that life is both real and very much worth while.

When I recollect I know that life is not static but expands unceasingly.

The mind's ability to recollect, to memorise, lifts the power of thinking and feeling on to the plane of permanency. Without memory, Man's life and being would become sterile and therefore useless. Memory, therefore, is a gift of the Spirit, precious beyond words, often misused, but ultimately containing the seeds of our salvation.

It is within memory's province to act as a guide and an inspiration both to thought and feeling; for good or ill as man's free will directs. Those three companions, thought, feeling, memory, form a Triad which in itself is the principal handmaid of the mind.

Perceived objectively, Memory appears to manifest in the form of countless transparent threads of light, both intertwined and single, housed and nurtured in a realm of their own creating; stretching backward into deep antiquity and also progressing in many forward ways.

We speak of 'living memory' as if memory had once been non-existent, but it is as eternally 'alive' as life itself. One of its outstanding qualities is the capacity to function both within and also beyond the range of time-matter-space conditions.

Great cosmic events, such for instance as the descent of the Christ spirit into human consciousness through the appearance of Jesus on earth levels, have never ceased from happening, and will continue until time is finally swallowed up in eternity: although such events seem to have occurred, once and for all, at a fixed moment in time and space.

Although man can now and again lose contact with his memory, memory is indestructible in itself and is also self-renewing.

The mind of man has not only the power to relive or revive memories from his own past, going back into the mists of his earliest existence as a 'man', but through training and under suitable circumstances, man's mind can use its memory to share the recollections of his fellow men and also those enshrined within the experiences of the Intelligences functioning inside those other Kingdoms of Nature by which we are surrounded.

Let us descend from the general to the particular in an effort to answer the question: 'How can I train my mind not only to bring specific memories to the surface of my consciousness, but also how can I become master of my memory and no longer remain its slave?'

Here is a simple exercise, a useful preliminary on the path leading to the recovering of personal recollections belonging to a period even before the beginning of one's present life on earth.

Think back to a specific moment in your youth or early maturity, pinpoint a particular experience or event that took place then. Follow intently the threads of memory relating to that specific experience or event as these threads spread backwards in human time and also as they flow forward.

Ponder upon the way in which these threads intermingle one with another, forming patterns of their own in the ever unfolding tapestry of your existence.

Try to follow these threads forward step by step until you arrive at the point in your present life at which you stand today. Then repeat the process in a backward direction from where you now are, and begin to comprehend how your present life and circumstances are indeed the direct and inevitable outcome of the summation of your every thought, word and deed over and throughout a period of 'time' immeasurable by human calculations.

Here is a useful hint.

Memory can be brought to the surface of the mind more easily during sleep when it is untrammelled by the complex activities of the brain. The brain is not the depository of memory although its etheric counterpart has associations with it. If you are interested in recovering recollection of some past experience, details of which seem to elude you, dwell with intent upon your desire immediately before sleep overtakes you. This is a valuable and a really worth-while form of discipline and training, and can yield interesting and even unexpectedly useful results.

A question I have been asked is this:

'In setting down a record of your memories connected with the time when Jesus walked the earth, how many of these recollections are claimed to be first hand and how many result from the sharing of the recollections of other people who happened to be alive at that time?'

I should like to be able to give a clear and concise answer to this query. I am aware that I can answer it to my own satisfaction, although incapable of putting this answer into words that would be understood by others. The narrative itself contains certain clues, indicating what may be termed direct and first-hand re-living of the events described, and in the second place what may be regarded as the thoughts and feelings of others who crossed my path.

Beyond that I cannot go.

In this matter, here is a word of warning, an important one. Whilst the Cosmic Record itself is exact, truthful, indestructible, one's personal recollections may at times prove faulty, incomplete or biased by wishful thinking or by particular quirks within one's human self.

I am no propagandist for my own infallibility.

However, I see no good reason why we should not share with one another the fruit of our individual recollections, because, in doing so, we may be allowed to help each other along the road that leads in the end to enlightenment and peace.

R.L.: To this reply, I have been permitted to add the following more personal (and characteristically modest) extract from a letter:

'The only way in which my life differs from the majority

of human lives is that I have disciplined myself, through life-long training, to develop that property of mind or consciousness through which the faculty of memory can be perfected and made available for use over and within long stretches in the unfoldment of human consciousness.'

The 'Glimpses'

W.T.P.: You ask me to describe Jesus' actual physical appearance. Everyone I have ever talked to describes him differently. Not at all surprising. When he was angry or indignant, Jesus seemed to grow visibly in stature; his eyes, his very features darkened, his whole personality underwent a change. Then again, when the Christ spoke through him, Jesus' body appeared to become luminous; his hair and his eyes lightened and he looked magnificent.

Myself I remember him as of medium height, around five feet ten inches, with blue-grey eyes that could become wells of incandescent darkness; with sun-tanned skin and hair of a rich brown with glints of gold in it; hair thick and crisp rather than curly, and cropped quite short, beautifully kept. It did not, at any time, go trailing over his shoulders. Later, when he grew a beard, it too was short, crisp, of the same colour as his hair. Long beards were rarely worn save by the elderly. Amazing that Jesus should have been so frequently depicted as somewhat effeminate, and usually as a man of forty years or more. Banish from your minds vision the misleading portraits that have come down to us. He retained youthful majesty and a virile beauty right up to the end of his life; even during his trial and on the Cross.

During part of that ordeal he was standing outside his physical form, and so was intermittently freed from agony. (Even we lesser mortals can do this, as I know from experience.) I do insist that not only his spiritual quality but his natural high spirits kept him vigorous and resilient throughout his life, despite the burdens he was forced to bear for those around him, as well as for the human race. Of course, during his last three years and a half, the overshadowing presence of the Christ carried much of the burden for him and protected him.

w.t.p.: An unforgettable glimpse of Jesus comes back to me. He has turned eighteen and is already slightly bearded. Whilst rambling along the banks of the Jordan (a bigger and deeper river in those days) Jesus spots a young hare lying wounded on the opposite bank of the river. I watch him, stripped and poised and upright, ready to dive in and swim across to the rescue. Standing there in the sunlight, vibrant with life and energy, he looks more like a young Greek god than the son of middle-class provincial Jewish parents. He gathers the wounded animal into his arms; and almost at once the hurt is healed and the hare bounds away in the joy of freedom regained. It is then that I notice the luminous magnetic aura which surrounds the hands of Jesus: a quality destined to serve him well throughout his healing ministry in the years to come. . . . On a subsequent occasion I was able to watch the way in which healing power radiated from his eyes.

I never met Jesus or any of those around him dressed in flowing garments like surplices, as most of his "portraits" would suggest. He usually wore a short linen tunic, sometimes loosely belted; beneath this a close-fitting under-tunic reaching from the waist to just above the knees, on a line with the over-tunic. His feet and ankles were beautifully proportioned and agile, and he often went about barefooted. Socks and stockings were not worn in those days, anyway by men: though now and then one met with fine closely-woven straw or fibre leggings, not unlike the modern puttee. Jesus never wore rings, amulets or any other ornament. In bad weather he wore a hooded cloak of camel-hair, which sometimes he wound round himself, giving the appearance of the kind of habit used by lay brothers in a monastery; and very occasionally he carried an olive-wood staff. But when he was walking or climbing he went cloakless, staffless, shoeless, with open tunic.

w.t.p.: Jesus was such a remarkable youth; it is amazing that he managed to remain free from public attention for so long.

r.l.: I suppose it was part of the 'Plan' that he should remain as it were veiled, anonymous almost, up to the time of his Baptism by John?

w.t.p.: Yes, no doubt he was kept 'hidden'. . . . But apart from that, people in those days weren't so alert, mentally alert. . . . Nowadays, it wouldn't be so easy.

r.l.: Joseph the father of Jesus is usually represented as a humble carpenter. Is this true?

w.t.p.: Not 'humble' by any means. He was a master carpenter, a master craftsman, comfortably off. . . . Mary his wife, the mother of Jesus, was a woman of refinement, country bred . . . tall, well-built, graceful. . . . Beautiful? No, not exactly. Good-looking. Wholesome. Good. She radiated goodness.

Mary of Magdala came from a family of culture and distinction. She was a beauty, and an accomplished singer and musician. She had never been a woman of the streets. At the age of nineteen she fell in love with an officer of the Roman Guard, stationed near Capernaum. Some time later, having completed his seven years of foreign service, her lover returned home to his wife and family in Ostia. This separation broke Mary's heart. She had left home to live with him, thereby disgracing herself in the eyes of her family, who cast her off. To earn her living she was obliged to sing and dance in the village taverns in Galilee and Jordan. It was at this period of her life that she met Jesus. The deep friendship that developed between them saved her reason and restored her self-respect. She became a healer in her own right, visiting leper settlements and working among neglected and orphan children. The illegitimacy rate was very high just then, because of the presence in Palestine of so many soldiers and foreign legionaries.

R.L.: Is it true that the parents of Jesus were Essenes?

W.T.P.: The Essenes had an inner core. Joseph and Mary didn't belong to that. They were rank-and-file Essenes. It was not from his parents that Jesus gained his esoteric Essene knowledge. That came much later, between his eighteenth and twenty-ninth year, when he paid several lengthy visits to one or other of their Retreats in the mountains around the Dead Sea. It was here that he was prepared for his mission of assuming the mantle of the Cosmic Christ.

R.L.: Is the Flight into Egypt an historical fact?

W.T.P.: That was before my day . . . some time before I had my connection with the boyhood of Jesus, or with his family. I haven't much doubt that this journey took place, although it is only recorded by St. Matthew. From time to time I had heard the story repeated, and there always seemed a sense of some mystery surrounding details. On one occasion I remember hearing a bereaved mother commenting: 'If only "They" had remained among us, the Hand of the Lord would have saved my son. And stayed the slaughter.'

Esoteric tradition speaks of a very holy Initiate of the Egyptian School of Mysteries whose blessing for Jesus Joseph and Mary sought. This sounds a rational explanation for taking such a long journey when Jesus was so young, apart from the reasons given in the Gospels.

W.T.P.: Jesus was such a passionate lover of the open air that he found it irksome to be tied to his father's carpentry. He was much closer to his uncle, Joseph of Arimathea, and spent a great deal of time with him both on his boats and in his lovely hill house, farms and gardens in Judea.

The stories about Jesus' visits to India, Britain and elsewhere are apocryphal, so far as I am aware. He did travel widely during sleep (as some of us lesser mortals are also able to do) and he may well have appeared in many places in the Orient in this way. . . . My recollections appear to indicate that on these occasions he met and spoke to many people, most of whom would be under the impression that they were in conversation with a holy man, clothed in actual bodily form.

When he was in his teens, he went on several journeys by sea with his uncle, thoroughly enjoyed himself away from home restrictions, and became an expert helmsman. His love for the sea, the wind and the sky knew no bounds. It is possible that he landed in Britain during one or more of these journeys. Certainly the legends of his having done so are very ancient and persistent. I would not like to deny them categorically.

w.t.p.: Jesus was a constant source of disquiet to his mother during his teens, owing to his habit if disappearing for days on end and then turning up without adequate explanation.

Yes, he had brothers, and at least one sister, so far as I can remember; and the house seemed always full of children. . . .

Relations between Jesus and Joseph his father were often a little strained. For one thing, Joseph had the craftsman's resentment of the kind of gypsy life led by his son for so long. He thought this mendicancy unworthy of the scion of a family claiming descent from the Royal Line of David, with Abraham as his distant ancestor. Because of this estrangement, Jesus spent much of his boyhood and youth on his uncle's estate. Had it not been for his uncle's generosity, Jesus and those who later gave up their living to follow him would often have been in sore financial straits.

The stories of bread and fishes galore were parables; and in my view the actual events on which they were based were by no means of the miraculous magnitude recorded in the Gospels.

Like all great Initiates, Jesus never performed miracles unless the need was urgent; or else for healing purposes. Never for self-healing. Only on rare occasions was he less than superbly healthy; but I remember one occasion when he was laid up with a severe bout of malaria. His symptoms were the usual ones, and he suffered from them and recovered in the ordinary way.

The answer to your question: Did he turn the water into wine, is yes, he did. This is a question of mentally sounding the right keynote. (I have helped to turn quite strong wine into pure water.) Whenever Jesus handled a jar of wine or oil, a cup, a platter, these objects and their contents became alive, scintillating, as if transformed. How lovely hands can be! Sure guides to character. How ugly, terrible even in their implications, are some human hands.

R.L.: Will you describe Joseph of Arimathea more fully?
W.T.P.: He was tall, muscular, strong, healthy . . . very intelligent. An extremely good speaker, almost an orator . . . possessed of the necessary personal magnetism. He was the owner of a merchant fleet and an expert in metal ores; a first-class farmer as well. A most astute business man . . . and charitable to a degree.

The mainspring of his emotional life was his burning love for his nephew throughout Jesus' whole life on earth and subsequently. I believe that the Talmud refers to him as Mary's uncle, and therefore great-uncle to Jesus. If this is accurate, it isn't easy to understand how he could still have been in the prime of life—as he certainly was— during Jesus' youth and early manhood. If the Talmud is correct, then the Arimathean must have been quite an old man when he settled in Avalon some years after the Cruci-fixion.

He had a son called Josephes who took over some of his father's merchant fleet. Josephes married in Cairo and subsequently went East.

Joseph was an influential member of the Sanhedrin—that is, the body that governed the religious life of the Jews, and was tolerated by the Romans: not only tolerated but respected.

For many years I was troubled by his absence from the Crucifixion—it seemed as if he had deserted Jesus at the supreme crisis of his earthly life; yet I only had to enquire in the right quarter to learn two salient facts: that Joseph of Arimathea (who in the beginning had never dreamed that the death penalty would be imposed) fought cease-lessly behind the scenes for a reprieve; and then at the last, was forcibly detained in Pilate's house in the City, because the authorities feared that his presence by the Cross would have unleashed a revolt.

w.t.p.: Jesus loved to sleep out of doors under the sky and the stars, quite unperturbed by wind, cold or rain. His custom was to rise early, while the rest of the world slept on, and go walking across the hills, up and down the valleys. Immense distances he covered in an incredibly short time; and he would turn up for the morning meal at the point of his departure, as fresh as when he started.

There was an occasion when I was allowed to accompany him on one of these dawn excursions. It took us along the upper reaches of the Jordan, north-east of the Lake of Galilee, and in the direction of snow-capped Hermon. Though young and hardy, I had much ado to keep pace with him. My breath came short; yet I was filled with inner restfulness and lapped in a peace beyond description. It was towards evening on this very occasion that I learned much of what, at long last, I am allowed to share with others: the true meaning of life and time and eternity; the irresistible power of selfless love; what compassion really means; the significance of the stillness of great silence; the oneness of life throughout the Seven Kingdoms of Nature and throughout the infinite majesty of all the Universes. . . .

Ah me!—how little I took in and really understood at the time! And how long it has taken even to attempt to fulfil what was laid upon me then!

w.t.p.: The early morning walk I referred to took place when Jesus was twenty-three, and therefore some time before the mantle of the Christ had fully clothed him. He was, of course, an Initiate in his own right; but during his youth he did not altogether comprehend the significance of the stupendous Overshadowing to come: not even when he met John the Baptist for the first time. All the legendary accretions of later years and centuries about his early life and his pre-baptismal days should be taken with a grain of salt. It is no part of my purpose either to affirm or to deny the doctrine of the Virgin Birth: only to state that *in those first days* there was no question of belief in either his or his mother's immaculate conception: no reason to think that his followers or his own family ever believed that his birth was in any way supernatural.

Tradition has it that there is a document still in existence written by Polycarp when he was acting as scribe to St. John on Patmos. (John could neither read nor write.) This is said to contain John's own memoirs dictated from memory when he was a very old man; and it will be found that there are no references in it to virgin births and the rest.

These writings are said to have been carefully inscribed on tablets of wax and, after Polycarp's passing, to have found their way into the hands of the Christian community in Athens. They were even smuggled into Rome. Much later they were lost or mislaid—having meanwhile been circulated to Christians in Smyrna and Antioch. Ultimately, it is thought, they came into the possession of the Empress Helena; and later still formed part of the Great Library assembled by the first Emperor Justinian.

A few years ago, when the Upper Room 'glimpse' reached me, it was indicated that the most accurate account of the Last or Seventh Supper was dictated by John to Polycarp. (John was the only disciple who truly understood the inner meaning of Jesus' acts and teachings.)

In my view, these unique tablets will one day be recovered; but apparently that time is not yet come. When it does come, certain strongholds of orthodoxy will indeed be shaken to their foundations.

w.t.p.: Returning once more to the days of Jesus, much in my mind at present: he usually spoke Aramaic, the colloquial tongue of the period. 'Thou shalt not' do this or that, for instance, would be worded differently, e.g. 'It is not seemly' to do this or that. It is only when Jesus' sayings were translated into Greek (and subsequently into Latin) that the denunciatory tone seems to have crept in. In Galilean Aramaic, the imperative was rarely if ever, used; or in any case never within my own knowledge.

I never heard Jesus use an imperative, even when speaking in Greek, as he occasionally did. But the merest suggestion on his part could create a sense of power, authority and certitude which could not be gainsaid.

When self-styled 'Teachers' communicate from the Invisible and use imperative or denunciatory language, it can be taken for granted that their degree of spiritual evolution is not a very high one.

w.t.p.: Do you know why the grain of mustard seed was used by Jesus in relation to the Kingdom of God? Not, in fact, because of its small size—there are many other types of seed smaller still. This is what I have been told: The mustard seed is the only known seed which is pure, in that it cannot be hybridised or grafted on to any other seed or plant of any other species than its own. In fact it is as inviolable as true faith itself.

r.l.: In a letter to w.t.p., discussing the sketchiness, the apparent contradictions and confusions in the four New Testament versions of the life of Jesus, I quoted one passage (in St. Mark's Gospel) which has always haunted my imagination. On the face of it, it is a simple, or rather bald statement of an odd, apparently irrelevant occurrence in the account of the arrest of Jesus; yet (I said) I had the impression that it was something else—something more in the nature of a clue, cryptically, deliberately planted, pointing to an event of the utmost significance in the drama.

'*And there followed him a certain young man, having a linen cloth about his naked body; and the young men laid hold on him. And he left the linen cloth and fled from them naked.*' (*Mark XIV* 51, 52.)

In his reply, w.t.p., remarks: 'The youth who fled ungarmented. I have been trying to trace his identity for you. A long trail finally led to his present whereabouts in his current existence. He asked me not to reveal his identity, for private reasons which he did not explain. . . .'

(I considered myself silenced by this totally unexpected answer. However, some weeks later, as will be seen, w.t.p. re-opened the subject of his own accord.)

What follows is a further extract from the same letter:

An exoteric and summarised version of the Akashic Records exists, and is sometimes tapped by truth seekers.

These exoteric records are not to be considered as material, bound and printed volumes existing in some secret vault or sealed subterranean cave on earth. They are a reflection, or a projection, on our ether, from the inner Akashic records. These latter are open only to spiritual, not to psychic vision.

The vibrations left on our planetary ether by the life and acts of Jesus are still strong, and can manifest in the form of a kind of television serial. People who happen to tap such a record often begin to identify themselves with this or that character in Jesus' entourage. If egocentrically inclined, they end by seeing themselves as actual participants. Quite a number of people alive today will assure you that they were, e.g. Peter, John, Mary Magdalene, etc. . . . irrespective of the fact that far more than one claimant exists for the self-same biblical character. (Should this be pointed out, the reply is apt to be: 'Oh, *the others* have all been deceived, of course, by bogus "Guides", or by their own wishful thinking!') This kind of aberration does not rule out the fact that many alive during Jesus' time *are* now once more on earth, as preparers of the Way for the fresh chapter in human history now beginning. You will never meet any true Initiate who will reveal his or her identity in any past life. It is against the rules to do so.

The Gospel narratives that have come down to us are not, of course, eye-witnesses' accounts of the events narrated. They are based largely on hearsay; sometimes on the memories of illiterate men and women incapable of writing for themselves. However, a mystery is involved here: namely, that on occasion the actual writers of the Gospels and also certain other New Testament recorders were 'overshadowed', and wrote inspirationally, in order that a fragment at least of truth might be passed down to future generations.

As an instance: Jesus, being an Initiate, would never have revealed to anyone details of his communion with and temptations by 'Satan', of which there were no eye-witnesses. Therefore the curious record we possess of such events has come down to us in the way I have described.

w.t.p.: I (the 'I' with whose mind, for the time being, the present writer had become completely identified) was little more than a boy when Jesus stayed a night or two with my parents; I being their only son. At that time we lived on a farmstead near Tyre. I spent most of my days working in our fields; occasionally fishing. I still remember how Jesus spoke and looked, and what joy he gave us all. It was long before he became renowned and was swallowed up among the multitudes. Towards sunset on the first day of his visit, he came out of the guest room where he had been praying, and told me to fetch a stool. We walked up to the village well, and he sat down beside it and asked me to fetch the children of our neighbours. As we sat around him, he began to tell us marvels, wonders . . . about birds, flowers, trees: how to speak to them and live with them; how, when he went swimming in Galilee and Jordan, he spoke to the fishes and entered into their natures and their lives.

Later my mother and many other women came to the well to fill their pitchers. Jesus helped them to draw up the water; he blessed the pitchers and the water they contained. My mother sent me to the inn to fetch my father and tell him to come home quickly and share with us the water blessed by Jesus.

I shall remember those two happy days to the end of time and beyond.

w.t.p.: No wonder his own family were often puzzled and estranged! Some of his remarks seemed to them to suggest that he felt no particular ties with them. Indeed, so loose were these ties that, as a boy, he would not be missed from the household until he had been absent for several days. If only Joseph of Arimathea had left some written record of Jesus' youth and early manhood; or had described his passionate love for the sea, and for boating and swimming; and how, on more than one occasion, he rode away for many days on caravan journeys, on a camel's back; and how he would withdraw alone, at certain seasons of the moon, into caves and high places, and return irradiated and refreshed! . . .

He was expert at ditching and draining the fields, and at gathering wild herbs for healing purposes as well as for the kitchen. In fact he revelled in every occupation pertaining to the creative side of farming: milking the cows, with Josephes for companion: tending the sheep: helping at calving time and lambing; ploughing with the oxen and the donkeys. All this, of course, while he was still Jesus the young man, the hidden Initiate, and long before the last three years of his life.

Often he helped to prepare and bake the unleavened bread in his aunt's kitchen. This bread, shaped into large flat scones that could be broken by hand (never cut) together with figs, and olives and green herbs, was his favourite diet. Meat and fish he cared not for; and wine only on ceremonial occasions. He would never fish for food, but he was often in communion with sea and river creatures and the very spirit of the waters.

I see him climbing the olive trees to beat down the fruit. I hear him laughing and shouting as the olives rain down on Josephes where he stands below. Then with a springing leap he has rejoined his cousin; and arm in arm, and gaily chattering, the two boys set out on a mountain climb.

R.L.: To my mind, one of the most arresting features of these 'glimpses' is the accent on high spirits, *joie de vivre*. This was constantly insisted upon after my saying that certain passages in the gospels conveyed the impression, not of a 'perfect man', but of a harsh, abusive, lamenting character who cursed unproductive specimens of the vegetable kingdom, kicked over tables, laid about him with a scourge of knotted rope, and drove that unfortunate herd of swine to their destruction. These examples of violent behaviour had, I said, much affected me in former days. They seemed to compose a portrait not wholly sympathetic; and anyway totally at variance with the gentle-Jesus-meek-and-mild, suffering-and-dying-for-us-miserable-sinners, tradition in which I had been brought up—or rather, left to flounder. The sense of the dichotomy had caused a mental stumbling-block almost as far back as I could remember; and had prevented me (and countless others, without doubt) from detecting, let alone appreciating, the power, the mystery, the staggering spiritual authority of some of his recorded acts and sayings. This 'Child with the sad name', as Jill Furze calls him in her haunting *Carol*, must sometimes have laughed or smiled . . . but only the Gospel of St. John gives even a hint of joy.

Here are some of w.t.p.'s comments and explanations:
As to the central Christian tenet that, through martyrdom, Jesus took our (human) sins upon his shoulders, and therefore presumably wiped them all out—such a belief would of course annul once and for all the Karmic law of cause and effect as applied to human life and conduct. Over and over again one comes across sincere and orthodox Christians who, after their departure hence, are horrified, aghast, to find that their own (Karmic) slates have not been wiped clean. For many such, Purgatory consists in the state

of shock and disillusionment into which they sink on finding that they alone are responsible for taking the essential steps through which 'salvation' can ultimately be attained.

As to the Temple incident: Jesus spoke out so strongly that after he had passed on into the Courtyard, some of his over-zealous followers returned into the Temple corridors and, without his sanction, began to overturn the tables, clash with the money-lenders, etc., thereby creating such a commotion that ultimately the Temple Guard intervened to restore order. In the melée, those responsible made their escape; but several of them were captured later, imprisoned for a while, scourged, fined and then released.

All these unseemly and untoward events were a cause of much concern to the Master; and resulted in his being followed and closely watched thereafter, both by the Jewish and the Roman authorities.

As to the cursing of the fig tree: neither the compilers of Luke nor of John thought this tradition worthy of mention. Jesus, being an Initiate, could live indefinitely on air and water, should the need arise. Reference to his being 'hungry' for material food such as figs is a most unlikely interpretation. This alleged incident took place just before the Passover, therefore before 15th March; and Jesus would, naturally, be well aware that not even the minutest fig would be visible in Palestine so early in the year. To curse a tree because it was unfruitful out of Nature's season is an act of which Jesus could not possibly be capable. . . . By the way, some oriental mythologies regard the grape and its fruit as symbolising spiritual enlightenment and joy; the apple or pomegranate as the container of both good and evil; and the fig as symbolising material and sensual knowledge and pleasure. However, I think the story that Jesus once cursed a material fig tree is pure myth.

As to the episode of the swine, Mark and John ignore this tradition or legend altogether. Evidently Matthew and Luke draw their information from the same source—although Matthew speaks of two men afflicted with devils in the Tombs (which were up in the mountains) and Luke mentions only one. Matthew, I think, speaks of a lake, and Luke of the sea; but no doubt they both had the Sea of Galilee in mind.

As to the swine, they were frightened by a cloud-burst, which (so far as I am aware) was purely coincidental: quite unconnected with the casting out of the unclean spirits. It is true that the unfortunate animals raced down a narrow ravine and were lost to sight; but it was miles from the sea! No one among the few onlookers present could read or write. The story, passed from village to village, each recipient adding some detail from his or her own imagination, could well be built up in after years—when the many stories of this kind about Jesus were beginning to be collated and recorded—to form the basis of the 'miraculous' accounts given in the Gospels.

One curious feature is that the 'devils' are said to have besought Jesus not to cast them into the 'deep'. According to pagan beliefs, all forms of life on this planet emerged from the sea. To be 'swallowed up in the sea' was equivalent to being returned to source for regeneration. Hebrews regarded swine as unclean creatures and their flesh was taboo to orthodox Jews. They would, however, be suitable as carriers to transport 'evil' spirits back to the 'sea' to be transmuted, and ultimately to emerge again, pure and regenerated. One can detect here the possible source of another of the elements in this strange episode, so much at variance with Jesus' character and teaching. I dare say one *could* unravel the complex strands and reach a final reasonable conclusion. . . . Personally I regard the stories both of the fig tree and the swine as largely apocryphal and partly symbolical.

Let me give you an autobiographical fragment to illustrate my meaning.

In 1918 I was instrumental in seeing that measures were taken to safeguard the lives of the Persian prophet Abdul-Baha and his family from possible martyrdom by the Turks when we were besieging Haifa and closing in on Mount Carmel, where the Bahai's had their settlement.

What I did could have been done by anyone else in my position (that of Staff Major in Intelligence) who had been able to discover the facts in time.

That incident happened less than fifty years ago; but in Persia and India it has already been converted into a miraculous legend. Followers of Abdul-Baha regard his spiritual status as equal to that of Jesus. In their records I have become a saint—one endowed with celestial powers and seership, through whose agency (and with much embroidery) their Master was saved from crucifixion by the Turkish military Governor of Haifa. I gather that these believers are now shown the 'exact spot' where the gallows were being erected at the time when we were storming the town.

Now, if in our modern times, with printing facilities, photography, the press, a considerable measure of literacy, an historical incident can be converted into a miracle worthy of Revelations, and within fifty years of the event itself, what might not have happened during the century or more after the time of Jesus with regard to what he actually said and did?—and before it was all written down, then copied from Aramaic into Hebrew, Greek and Latin; then re-copied and annotated over and over again, each copyist adding his own gloss or his pre-conceived 'interpretation'? The wonder is that we are left with anything at all which can rightly be regarded as authentic.

All that concerned Jesus was that his teachings and his life-work should be 'inscribed in Heaven'—that is, indelibly, eternally imprinted upon the Akashic Tablets of Life. He never wrote down anything himself. The teachings of the Christ in him were universal, for all time: generalisations on such a cosmic scale that they can be applied anywhere, in any period of earth's history.

w.t.p.: There was an occasion, soon after the first disciples had been chosen and brought together, which stands out in my memory: although I do not think that any of the four Gospels refer to it directly. It was at sunset, on the seashore not far from Capernaum, when Jesus was telling them of the great events with which they would soon be associated. Among much else of profound and prophetic interest, Jesus made a statement that caused consternation to his hearers. He warned them that a new era was about to dawn; and that the Lamentations of the venerated Hebrew prophets were a closed book, no longer to represent authority or even to exact obedience for the future.

At that time the disciple nearest to Jesus was Simon (Peter); and therefore it was Simon who voiced the general consternation when he heard Jesus apparently belittling the status and the permanent value of what we now call the Prophets of the Old Testament. Such talk sounded alarmingly heretical to Jews nurtured on the Sacred Books of their ancestors.

Seeming to ignore their disquiet, Jesus went on to tell them about the Book of the New Age, whose contents were destined to supersede all that had gone before. To an on-looker it appeared as if, in his state of exaltation, Jesus was actually predicting the descent of the Kingdom to earth levels within the life span of his followers.

He spoke of the Footstool of his Father as if this were, in reality, the world we live in; inferring that those who learned how to climb upon it to kiss the feet of God would at once find themselves in Heaven. Certainly Simon, and several others, became convinced that they were shortly to witness the descent of the Kingdom of Heaven, with their Master as its Sovereign Ruler.

How natural that they failed to understand that Jesus was speaking of—and to—the future; a future thousands of years distant, when men would once more begin to become in truth the children of God!

On a later occasion, also at sunset, near the Lake, during one of the Seven Suppers, Jesus spoke at length about the way in which men born of the flesh of their parents could be re-born in spirit even while still on earth. It was Andrew who questioned him about his (Jesus') own birth and all the rumours current in the air. Jesus replied that the Christ Spirit which had entered into him 'that scripture might be fulfilled' heralded the time when all mankind would be lifted up and redeemed by the same experience; the time when men and angels would walk the earth together as the sons and daughters of the one God.

Again, those that heard him misinterpreted his words, assuming that this hour was soon to strike. To the onlooker, and in the light of history, it is no wonder that in the early days of their training the disciples were often baffled and perplexed.

Jesus never seems to have made it clear to them when he was speaking as an individual to individuals, and when the Christ was speaking through him—not so much to those present as to the countless generations yet unborn. In the middle of a conversation often about everyday affairs, his countenance would change, his delivery become compelling, authoritative. Then the words that issued forth would be addressed to all mankind in all the ages. . . . But those who were actually listening went on applying his prophecies and statements solely to themselves and to their own generation.

I am speaking, of course, of the three years at the close of his short life when the Christ clothed and permeated his whole being. In earlier years he was very much a man among men, speaking a language they could understand, often eloquent, inspiring, but always simple. Not until he met John the Hermit (Baptist) did the immensity of the mission which lay ahead begin to dawn and then gradually to encompass him.

Right up to his tragic end, John was never really sure whether this man whom he had baptised among so many others was that One whose imminent coming he, the Baptist, had looked for and predicted.

I feel certain that there are records still in existence, awaiting discovery, which make clear the mystery of the Master's seemingly dual personality, and elucidate the change that took place within him in the waters of the Jordan, in his twenty-eighth year.

w.t.p.: Jesus the man had been prepared for aeons for his destiny, not only on this planet. He has never been reborn except as himself. By this I mean that when he assumes a physical form and comes and goes in it (for some particular purpose) this form is as it were anonymous: never the body of some historic personage.

No true Initiate, when he adopts a body for temporary use, labels himself with an earthly name or personality. Others who sit at his feet may give him a title for use among themselves; but that is different.

These are two orders of embodiment through which an Adept can manifest.

1. By the willing assumption of ordinary physical birth.
2. By assuming a bodily robe as and when the need arises.

After his great Overshadowing Jesus underwent a permanent extension of auric potency; so much so that 'segments' of this potency can be reflected through humble and saintly beings like St. Francis; or Padre Pio; or for that matter Pope John XXIII, and many others far too numerous to mention.

w.t.p.: You have heard or read somewhere that Jesus was congenitally lame? Nonsense. . . . It is true that when he was fifteen he barked his shin during a storm at sea in one of his uncle's ships en route from Jaffa to Alexandria. He was learning to handle the helm at the time. The resultant lameness lasted some weeks, but never returned; (though he did appear to be a little lame when carrying the Cross uphill, at the close of his earthly life).

The scribes and Pharisees brought a woman who had been caught in the act of committing adultery, and making her stand forward they said to him: 'Teacher, this woman was caught in the very act of committing adultery. Now Moses has commanded us in the Law to stone such creatures; but what do you say?' ... Jesus stooped down and began to write with his finger on the ground; but as they persisted with their question, he raised himself and said to them: 'Let the innocent among you throw the first stone at her'; then he stooped down again and wrote on the ground. (John. Chapter 8, New English Bible.)

Presumably (I wrote, R.L.) this mystifying act of Jesus was in the nature of a response of some kind—was relevant to the situation and the question? But how? Superficially, the passage reads either as if he were giving himself time to think, knowing that the question was a trap; or possibly, as if he might have been 'making white magic' to protect himself. But neither of these interpretations seems to point to the reality; and the picture of Jesus stooping, writing, vibrates in the imagination with undertones of something in it far beyond our normal comprehension.

'He wrote in hieroglyphs', replied w.t.p., not letters; and what he wrote has not yet been revealed. Though simple in essence, it would have been too esoteric in its implications to register with those present on that occasion. Although virile in the fullest human sense, Jesus never shared sexual experience with any other person during his life on earth; and for this reason it would have been difficult, perhaps impossible, even for him, to enter into complete understanding of the insidious compulsion of sexual temptation for the majority of those around him. Undoubtedly, however, he was aware of the immense pressures resulting from Nature's insistent urge to ensure propagation of the species throughout the Seven Kingdoms; and at all times he was deeply concerned with the problem of sex, and with the ceaseless conflict between man's higher nature and his lower; also with the double standard of morality, as prevalent in his times as it is today.

In my view, Jesus desired to make sure, as the result of this Act of Writing, that his attitude towards sexual morality as well as the example set by his personal purity should become permanently engraved on human consciousness. Through the action he took, the assurance given to the woman taken in adultery would be rendered more durable in its effects. He was impregnating the ground with a certain thought impulse. Having been thus 'earthed' it could become available and effective—not immediately, not within a period to be measured in centuries of earth time; but in terms of 'that far-off divine event to which the whole Creation moves'.

It was an immense, a cosmic act.

It is reasonable to suggest that sex, as we know it, is a comparatively temporary phase in the evolutionary process as a whole.

For a countless period of time after the human form had emerged from purely animal structure, it contained only a primitive soul entirely subject to animal instincts and sensations. The life essence even then belonged to the

Eternal Order of Being, but was not imbued with any individualised intelligence of its own. No records, historical or legendary, remain to inform us of the descent into matter of the first great Messenger sent out through the Creative Hierarchy to earth levels by divine command. His name and his mission are lost in the mists of time; and he has long since passed beyond and above the confines of our solar system. But it is permissible to indicate that the main object of his coming was to bring with him conditions through which what we call the human soul could begin to occupy the bodily forms which had hitherto been animal in function. (Some seers believe that this 'descent' marked an event that has since been described as the First Fall.) In any case, and no doubt for evolutionary purposes still unrevealed to us, this descent engendered that duality of action which has led to the seemingly inevitable conflict between man's animal being and his human self; a dilemma which still remains the dominating factor in the life experience of all of us.

It was at that incalculably distant past in history that the separation of the sexes came about. This sex division, with its corollary of struggle between sense and super-sense (or Spirit), is hard for us to understand. Sex, which in this world can be the supreme way back to unity, and thus to eternity, is also the supreme obstacle.*

Considering the problem from another, a non-metaphysical angle, one is led to suppose, that, before this seemingly catastrophic separation came about, all forms of life upon this planet had been without sex differentiation

*cf. William Blake: '*The sexual garments sweet*
Grow a devouring winding sheet'.

as we understand it, yet capable of self-reproduction.

It was clear to Jesus' prophetic vision when he was on earth that the human race had to plunge even further into materialism and sensuality before the limit of the downward arc was reached, and the swing upward in the evolutionary cycle could begin. For this reason he could only teach in language simple in itself yet permeated with the leaven of the fundamental principles upon which all life processes and progressions are based. Man was—is—destined to drain to the dregs the cup that he himself has fashioned and filled with sorrow, suffering, selfishness, greed, envy, fear and every conceivable sexual and emotional excess and deviation.

The downward plunge into matter could not be halted by the Incarnation of Jesus the Christ; it still had over two thousand years to run before the upward swing could begin to be impelled—largely out of the tragedies consequent upon diving into the mud and mire of materialism at its densest. As an example of this strange process of descent into the lowest depths, one knows of men and women who have deliberately undergone every possible sexual and other degradation as a seemingly necessary preliminary to the attainment of ultimate salvation.

To very few was Jesus able to explain why it would have been useless to give out to the multitudes more than they could accept. He was well aware that to his Successors would fall the task of spiritual revelations far beyond and above what he himself was permitted to impart. For this reason it is important to begin to seek and to unveil the 'pearls' of wisdom and understanding that Jesus demonstrated by his aura and by his example rather than by his 'words' alone.

.p.: There is an esoteric tradition to the effect that on an occasion in Jesus' thirty-first year on earth, during a time of great restlessness in the political and social atmosphere around him, a few close to him heard the following words above the din and clamour of an unruly and hostile mob outside the Damascus Gate on market day: 'I say unto you, whatever your deeds may be, let them be done in My Name, that you may enter the Kingdom and find rest.'

Of course Jesus never made utterances of this kind on his own responsibility. 'My Name' referred to the Eternal Christ by whom Jesus was overshadowed.

Like so many of the sayings which have come down to us more or less intact, there is a depth of meaning in this utterance which far transcends the words employed. We are to bring 'the Christ' right down into every detail of our lives; our thinking and feeling, our doing and acting; our relationship both with our inner selves and outwardly with all our fellows. We are commanded to imprint 'My Name' on everything we do; our eating and drinking, our conversations and communications, our business and our recreations; all our acts of living and loving, whether low or exalted, whether ignorant or enlightened.

In fact *nothing* we think, say or do should be thought, said or done until we have implanted in it by an act of will the imprimatur of 'My Name'—the sign manual of the Christ, and those great principles which in themselves are the Christ. In this way, by divine grace, our sins and all the seeming darkness in us—all—all—through our own act of will can become stepping stones out of the gloom and mire up into the light of a new day.

w.t.p.: There were three occasions during the first year of his Ministry when Jesus spoke to five of his disciples on problems of sex, and on the earthward gravitational impulses of the natural man. Teaching was given on esoteric methods whereby the forces behind all sex impulses could be transformed and transmuted into spiritual energy. But in spite of the mystification and disappointment of those present, Jesus enjoined secrecy in regard to what he told them about the application of these methods. Beyond their comprehension was the realisation that the law of cause and effect in human evolution could not be halted or sidetracked; and that this law was destined to be worked out through the descent of man still further into the abyss as the only route left open to him that would actually, and ultimately, lead to the first step upwards.

We may confidently expect the coming Messenger from God to throw a flood of light on sexual problems and their solution.

As to your question about magic. 'White magic' is simply the operation of spiritual law in human affairs, unobstructed by man-made ignorances and frictions. Because we know so little about the working of the Law, when we see a demonstration of its operation we call it magic; whereas it is spiritually natural, and will ultimately become universal.

Man-made magic, largely induced by rituals, bloodletting and sexual practices unharnessed: all this is *not* in line with the evolutionary process. It can be fascinating, but also degrading; apt to induce the artificial release of repressed emotions and desires; dependent largely on the use of astral fluids—which can be potent, but which are essentially unstable, and therefore unreliable. Neither Jesus nor any other great Initiate ever descended to such practices.

The astral realms are fluid. A mere breath of motion at once disturbs these fluids, and causes distortion and mis-calculation. . . . Rarely nowadays is there any true serenity and stillness within our fluidic-astral 'worlds'; hence the unreliability of communications through this medium.

The human intellect alone is incapable of arousing man's creative imagination, or of bringing it into full flower. Orderly evolution, and the striking of the correct balance between the use of the mind and the feelings can lead naturally to the point at which spiritual enlightenment unfolds. When this happens, psychic vision to the extent needed (if at all) becomes the natural corollary and maid-servant of spiritual seership. Then all is well.

But magicians are apt to seek short cuts towards the generation of psychic power—mainly through the abnormal stimulation of the imagination at the expense of man's mental and spiritual development and progress. Certain drugs, the specific use of alcohol, abnormal breathing exercises are among the artificial methods by which the creative imagination can be first aroused, then activated. Sex can also be utilised for the same purpose. The etheric counterpart of semenal fluid (an invaluable creative sub-stance when properly employed) is the medium through which man's imagination mainly operates within our three-dimensional world; and indeed upon etheric and astral levels as well. The rituals employed during sexual orgies depend upon the phases of the moon, and can be carried out between the sexes, homosexually, or in individual units.

A series of orgasms, whether produced by intercourse or artificially, can bring about the release of the emotions from all mental control. A kind of lower astral ecstasy, usually mistaken for 'enlightenment' through psychic visions, is thus achieved. It is easy to understand the exhilaration, the sense of blissful freedom from the domination both of the mind and of the senses experienced by those thus freed from all spiritual safeguards.

To empty oneself in order to be filled from the divine reservoir is a purely mental process strongly to be encouraged—subject to safeguards aimed at preventing the possible creation of a vacuum. On the other hand, the artificial practice of emptying oneself emotionally by the forcible expulsion of the totality of the semenal fluids, both physical and etheric, can (at best) only induce illusory and sensual dreams which are the exact opposite of true psychic and spiritual enlightenment.

R.L.: I had neither received nor expected to receive any further information about the young man of St. Mark's Gospel who slipped out of his linen cloth and fled naked; but after the lapse of many weeks, and with an effect of dropping a piece of casual information into an otherwise 'ordinary' letter, W.T.P. wrote:

'Your young man was virile, and possessed a particular kind of magnetism with which the linen robe he wore had become imbued. It was this linen cloth that was used to preserve the etheric double whilst Jesus was in the Tomb. In fact, it was a major portion of the cerements. Now, nothing happens "by accident"; the details of all cosmic events affecting human destiny are prepared for centuries before they take place outwardly. When he touched Jesus, your young man had a sudden overwhelming vision of the horrors of the approaching tragedy—more than he could stand. Casting off the garment, he fled, not even knowing of the service he had been destined to render Jesus.'

R.L.: Once again, to be 'touched' by these few lines was to receive a kind of electric shock. It was as if, after years of fruitless scanning and searching, I had at last seen that nameless, faceless, stripped figure of a young man focussed in a night-piercing telescope, self-illumined by the unique meaning of his life. Was it because I had already, very tentatively, dared to surmise a possible link between the shed garment and the grave-clothes that my intuition acquiesced spontaneously? No; surely the story itself, 'so huge, so hopeless to conceive', and at the same time so natural, one might say almost pedestrian, compels attention.

What follows is an attempt to make a whole of W.T.P.'s subsequent comments and descriptions; without, of course, changing the essential content of his narrative.

W.T.P.: The Garden is full of shouting and tumult, of comings and goings to and fro. It is a dark night, and the soldiers around the Captain of the Guard of the High Priest, who has come to arrest Jesus, are carrying torches and lanterns as well as arms. They form a ring round Jesus and his immediate followers, and strive to keep back the milling crowd beyond: for the news has spread through the city and out into the suburbs, and the throng thickens, quickens, heavy with rumour, muttered assertion, contradiction.

Now, seized by panic terror, Jesus' friends desert him. He is alone.

As I watch, a tall youth, dark and handsome (not, I think a Jew), splashes his way across the Brook and presses forward until he reaches the outskirts of the crowd. I hear him asking what is going on; but no one seems to know how to answer him. Then, as if suddenly impelled, he battles his way forward through the press of onlookers and soldiers until he stands before Jesus; touches him on the breast. So soon as this is done, he cries aloud, and, leaving his fine-woven linen garment at Jesus' feet, flees away naked in a kind of frenzy, leaping and shouting furiously. The crowd seems momentarily to dissolve, aghast, to let him through.

It is borne in upon me that this young man is well-bred and educated, but that his family have cast him out because of his strange ways, and his apparent power of divination. Evidently it is this gift which enables him, on touching Jesus, to receive the reflected impact of the tragic events about to be. Still crying and lamenting loudly, he dashes up the slopes of Mount Scopus, driven by the instinctive urge to escape from his vision by flight into the wilderness.

The officer of the Guard, shaken, and fearing that in some way this incident presages an attempt to rescue Jesus, commands one of his men to pursue, capture alive and at all costs bring back the apparently demented fugitive. The name of this soldier is Kopul. Rapidly shedding his mail and his heavy footwear in order to move more quickly, he picks up the discarded garment, slings it over his shoulder and sets off. But the light sandals he had thrust on in haste soon become filled with grit, and painfully impede him as he races through olive groves, through harsh scrub and spiny cactus towards the bare rock summit.

On one who at that moment happened to be riding within the mind of the pursuer, Kopul, incidents connected with that chase left an indelible impression. It was as if the linen garment acted as a mysterious emotional link between the hunter and the hunted. The terror and desolation driving the distraught youth blindly onwards invade the breast of Kopul to the exclusion of all else. One urge alone obsesses him: to catch up with his quarry, share his grief, console him.

All through the night that chase went on, down through the cactus-covered waste lands and on into the sombre valley leading towards Jericho and the Dead Sea. Finally, just before dawn, Kopul gives up, defeated: he has lost all sense of direction in the trackless wilderness. Slowly, slowly, crawling, exhausted, pain-racked, full of foreboding, he makes his way back to the Garden of Gethsemane.

The dawn is breaking, the crowds have disappeared, there is no sign of Jesus or of his companions, or of the Sanhedrin priests and guards. Only despair is abroad, a presence almost palpable, brooding in the emptiness.

I seem to be sharing with Kopul a feeling of terror, frustration, and utter loneliness. Still carrying the young man's robe, he leaves the garden, crushed by the sense of some failure graver, more profound by far, than failure in his military duties. I follow him and his thoughts with much interest. His first impulse is to go into the city market and sell the robe which, being of the finest linen, would certainly fetch a high price. Then he changes his mind and decides to return to barracks to report before going on leave. He removes his stained soiled uniform, washes, dons civilian garb, and sets out to look for Mary of Magdala.

Another series of flashes gives me the clue to the link between Mary and this Jewish soldier. Years earlier he had been seconded for liaison purposes to the troop commanded by the Roman officer who became Mary's lover. It was in this way that he met her; and later during the time of Mary's devoted service to the Master, they became fast friends. Kopul admired her for her pluck and ready wit.

It is while carrying the linen garment towards the market place that Mary comes into his mind. I see him searching the city for her; indeed he goes on searching all that day. Later he finds her walking the streets, distraught, unable to discover what has become of Jesus since his arrest the night before. (She had not been present in the Garden.) She listens eagerly to the story Kopul tells her and gratefully accepts the garment.

When all was finished and Jesus crucified, Joseph of Arimathea secured the custody of his nephew's body. He asked Mary Magdalene and two others to accompany him in arranging for the burial rites. Mary brought with her the linen garment which had so recently come into her possession. Thus it fulfilled its destiny and became a portion of the Shroud. Permeated as it was with the strong and vital magnetism of its original wearer, it proved invaluable by acting as a kind of balm for Jesus' body. The terrible mutilations he had inevitably suffered during the Crucifixion naturally affected the rhythm of his etheric counterpart. The 'power' in this particular garment helped to restore the rhythm, thus making it easier for his subtle form to emerge; also facilitating the rapid disintegration or dematerialisation of the physical body for which Jesus had no more use.

Very rarely do angels appear in human form; but the Angels of the Passing, dedicated to Jesus' service, did so in order (among much else) first to remove the napkin from his head.

That napkin constituted, of course, a ceremonial portion of the last earthly rites performed for Jesus with ineffable love, grief and reverence. Its removal was part, you might say, of the angelic rites designed to assist his ethereal body to emerge. The angels even took the trouble to fold the napkin and place it in a secluded spot 'by itself' and 'specially wrapped together'!

There is deep significance behind every incident of this kind recorded in the Gospels.

On the third day, when Jesus appeared before Mary, his warning: 'Touch me not' signified (I have been allowed to gather) that his new and more spiritual form had not yet become sufficiently stabilised to be able to endure a human contact without damage to its supra-physical rhythm. A touch would have gone right through it, hurtfully. Later, however, when he had returned more fully into physical conditions, during the forty days, it is recorded (by Mark) that he appeared to his disciples 'in a different guise'; by Matthew that they 'clasped his feet'; by John that he invited Thomas to 'reach your finger here; see my hands: reach your hand here and put it in my side; be unbelieving no longer, but believe'.

Judas Iscariot; the Role of Lucifer; and other Matters

ONE OF THE problems that puzzles me is connected with the rôle that Judas is reputed to have played just before Jesus' arrest. For over a year previously, the Master's words, actions, movements had been carefully noted by the Roman and Jewish intelligence network. Jesus went openly about the country and was a well-known figure, easily recognisable, and regarded as a potentially dangerous political agitator both by the Government and by the Sanhedrin authorities. The military contingent sent by the High Priests to compass his arrest needed no intervention by Judas or anyone else to enable them to mark their man. In any case, among the crowd that had gathered in the Garden were many who could have pointed unerringly to Jesus. Why therefore were Judas' services required? Did the incident of the kiss, if it is authentic, act out the fulfilment of part of some prophetic ritual? . . . I cannot write of this problem from first-hand experience.

(Incidentally, there were no visible signs to suggest that the 'High Priests and Elders of the People' were present in the Garden to supervise the arrest. The armed emissaries acting that night on their explicit orders appeared to number at least one hundred officers and men.)

Few alive today will be able to understand the rôle of Lucifer as an essential background to the Christ's ministry on earth through Jesus. Those who do will begin to grasp the enigma of Judas' life and actions, and the way in which 'darkness' was used, to throw into constructive relief the Light of the Christ message to the human race.

In our outer world of life and being, the Light contained in Truth or the Truth contained in Light can only be recognised by us through or against a background of contrasting darkness. Dominated as we are by our dualities, by the action of energies opposed to one another, we learn how to recognise what is called 'good' by contrasting its manifestations with what appears to us 'less good' or 'bad'.

Lucifer is the 'fallen' angel who was willing to descend into the material darkness of human consciousness on earth; the Light-Bearer who is also the Prince of Darkness, and in the ultimate sense Christ's true collaborator. His 'disciples' are Intelligences that operate through their influence on human consciousness or through the mass consciousness; and manipulate, control the negative forces in order that the positive forces may rise up. Our conception of Lucifer as fearsome, 'evil', 'The Enemy', is surely narrow and distorted. Cosmically speaking, Christ and Lucifer are, symbolically, opposite sides of one and the same coin, because Absolute Light and Absolute Dark are bound to contain one another. Thus Lucifer may well be as much an instrument of divine purposes as the Christ himself. *'I Jesus have sent mine angel to testify unto you these things. . . .'*

Lucifer incarnate in humanity can be regarded as a kind of celestial leaven: he can only 'arise and go unto his Father in Heaven' as humanity itself arises. To regain the placè he sacrificed in the spiritual realms Lucifer must bring us with him: hence the references in Eastern scripts to this great Being as both Tempter and Redeemer.

The presence of Judas the Iscariot among the disciples chosen by Jesus was no accident—no irretrievable or inconceivable blunder on his part. From the scanty records that have come down to us it might seem that the selection of the disciples was a casual, spontaneous affair. On the contrary: we may be sure that each of those who were to become his close followers and daily companions was chosen with deep prophetic insight for a special purpose, in order to fulfil a pre-determined destiny—one which he alone was able to fulfil.

For reasons which doubtless go back into aeons of past time, it was Judas' fate to be cast for the rôle of Enemy, of grossest, purblind plunger in the mire of self-destruction during the last tenebrous period of Jesus' life on earth. His Act of Darkness could be thought of as an impenetrable backcloth against which the Light of the Christ, of Christ's universal message, shone out by contrast with wider and more intense effulgence.

Jesus must of course have known from the beginning that Lucifer, the supreme tester of human minds and hearts, was destined to carry out his mission through Judas at that particular moment in world history: and that Peter also would come under the spell of Lucifer and temporarily succumb. We may think it strange that in both these instances, while forecasting the outcome, Jesus did not intervene—since it was in his power to do so—and so change the current of events: but we may be sure that purposes of stupendous import were being fulfilled through the cosmic interplay of Light and Darkness, Light within Darkness, which constituted the dramatic essence of Jesus' life on earth within our midst.

Apart from such matters *sub specie aeternitatis*, the effect of Judas' remorse and tragic end must have done much of importance to strengthen the moral and spiritual fibre of the Christian martyrs from that time onwards. The supreme example, perhaps, of good coming out of evil.

R.L.: I began at last to see that it was possible to think of Judas as one whose tragic rôle was a necessary element contributing to the final ineffable catharsis: as Jesus' dark brother.

Some weeks later came this story in a letter.

W.T.P.: *Judas:* I must speak as if through a veil—on the lines of *The Upper Room*—and I am relying upon memory rather than on the capacity to 're-live' the experience in so far as I was concerned with it.

It happened one bitter winter evening during the second year of Jesus' public ministry. A protégé of mine was a young Syrian of eighteen, Reuben by name, who showed signs of becoming a very remarkable singer and musician. Never before or since have I heard such a strong, clear and lovely tenor voice. I had helped to finance his training, and his parents were old friends of mine. His home was near Damascus; but on the occasion to which I am now referring, this young man had come down to meet me in Capernaum, where I was staying at the time. On the evening in question I had invited a few friends to join me at the inn where I was lodged, to give them the pleasure of hearing Reuben's glorious voice.

One of these good friends brought with him Judas the Iscariot. I had met him only twice before, when he had impressed me as a man of culture and intelligence; he was musical besides.

It was a wonderful evening, for Reuben was in exceptionally good voice. He sang hill-country shepherd songs, and chanted several of the most inspiring Songs of David in a prophetic and enthralling manner.

When the party was breaking up, Judas drew me on one side, saying that he wanted to ask my advice. He then showed me a piece of gold in the form of a medallion; and, knowing that I was an authority on Roman coinage, asked me its origin and value. It turned out to be a specimen of the medallion struck by the City of Rome for presentation to those who received the Freedom of the City in return for outstanding services.

Judas told me that, only the night before, Mary of Magdala had given him this coin to buy a warm cloak for Jesus, who, he told me, was at present staying near Capernaum. Two days before, late in the afternoon, Jesus had been asked to go up into the hills behind the town to rescue a shepherd boy who had been found suffering from the effects of several days and nights of exposure after breaking a leg; and was now too sick to be moved. Everyone in Galilee knew of Jesus' immense love for shepherds and for all those responsible for the care of animals.

Judas told me that he was with Jesus when the summons came; and that he had arranged for the shepherd's two older brothers to accompany Jesus, taking with them a rough wooden stretcher. Two other members of the household also went along, to act as guides and helpers. When Jesus reached the spot he took off his cloak and wrapped the boy, now semi-unconscious, in its ample folds.

It was then that the miracle occurred. No stretcher was needed; the boy stood up in full possession of his senses, able to climb down the rugged mountain-tracks unaided, the broken leg mended and straightened. Having arranged for one of the brothers to return into the hills and mind the sheep, Jesus blessed the boy and sent him home still with the cloak around his shoulders.

When Mary Magdalene heard what had happened, she gave Judas this golden coin and begged him to sell it to provide Jesus with a new cloak. According to Judas, the medallion was a parting gift to Mary from the Roman officer whom she had loved so passionately. It was an infinitely precious memento; and nothing but the thought of Jesus cloakless on that bitter winter night would have induced her to part with it. But, said Judas, the community purse was empty, Joseph of Arimathea absent overseas: accordingly he had felt obliged to accept her gift. Since it was impossible to use the medallion as currency, could I help him to find a purchaser?

I explained that it would be contrary to Roman law to barter or sell a gold piece of this description; and I insisted that it should be returned forthwith to the giver. I then remembered that my father had given me a very warm camel-hair cloak as a birthday present, and that I had scarcely worn it since. I sent my servant to fetch it from my home in the outskirts of Jerusalem, with instructions to give it to Mary, so that she could alter it for Jesus, whose figure differed from my own. . . . Memory of further details fades at this point; but I do remember, with great joy, that when I met Jesus some time later, my cloak was around his shoulders.

There is a strange sequel, nearly nineteen hundred years later, to this story. In the early winter of 1919, when I was walking with Abdul-Baha Abbas on Mount Carmel, he noticed that I was suffering from the cold. Immediately he took off his camel-hair cloak and threw it round my shoulders.

At that time I had forgotten the incidents recorded in these notes, and therefore could not understand what the wind seemed to be whispering in my ears: '*Restitution after many days . . .*'.

w.t.p.: Let us take a page out of Jesus' uncomplex Book of Life! Wisdom is not generated from occult theories and speculations, or metaphysical intricacies. So many earnest students and pilgrims eagerly pursuing the path of knowledge find themselves bogged down and lost in alluring by-ways that end in cul-de-sacs. The spiritual road to progress is a simple one, not cluttered up by a mass of non-essentials.

Simplify! Simplify!!

Jesus still surrounds himself with very simple people,

many of whom might even fall into the category you have correctly assigned to you and me—namely, 'Worms'. (Deliberate falsification. R.L.) In any case it is rarely the seemingly likely people who are chosen for his work.

w.t.p.: *Stephen.* Of all the throng that followed later in Jesus' footsteps, only Stephen could begin to compare with Jesus in physical perfection. He was a rare and lovely soul, and a natural Seer, seemingly cut off before his time. Even after Saul had (for personal reasons known to me) become his enemy and refused to save him from death by stoning (see The Acts of the Apostles, Chapter 8, *And Saul was consenting unto his death*) he said to Saul: 'We shall meet again, and as friends. Not only in another world, but in this . . .', adding the cryptic statement, perhaps in reply to some bitter or scornful comment on the part of Saul: 'When the very stone that slayeth me shall have seven eyes'.

I take this to mean that the time will come when even the so-called lowest kingdom, the mineral, will be lifted up and become spiritually possessed of the vision of the Unity of Life eternally present in all the Seven Kingdoms of Nature.

I was not present at the stoning of Stephen (though afterwards in touch with him), and therefore my information is not first hand. . . . I believe that Zechariah writes of a stone with seven eyes as presaging the Golden Age of universal brotherhood.

The writings of Zechariah, comparatively new at the time, caused much disputation and discussion in the temples and synagogues of Palestine when Stephen was a boy. This might possibly account for his strange allusion. Can you verify it?

R.L.: The passage I was asked to verify runs thus:

For behold the stone that I have laid before Joshua; upon one stone shall be seven eyes: behold, I will engrave the graving thereof saith the Lord of Hosts. (Zechariah, Chapter 3. A portion of his prophecy of the coming of Christ or *The Branch*.)

W.T.P.: *The Mystery of the many 'Johns' of the Gospels.*

Many years ago, long before I took any special interest in the subject, I was shown in a flash the relationship between the various Johns mentioned in the New Testament.

The name John was a favourite one in the days of Jesus, and many Hebrew boys received it as a second name when a different first name had been already chosen. This second name was used on ceremonial occasions, as one means of differentiating them from the normal life of every day, when the first name would be in use. For instance, at the Feast of the Passover, any boy in the household bearing the name of John (whether primary or secondary) would be so addressed.

There was one John whose first name was Simon. He was a kinsman of Joseph of Arimathea, and lived and served on the estates after having failed in his own affairs and become bankrupt. He was a devotee of Jesus unmentioned in biblical records; one whose love for Jesus was so deep that he would gladly have died for him. He it was who was sent by the Arimathean to try to help Jesus carry the Cross on the way to Calvary. He it was who helped to safeguard the welfare of the three Marys present at the Crucifixion;

to whom Jesus entrusted his mother; who took her to his home when all was over.

Unless the fragment left of my 'recollection' is deceptive, it was he who ran with Peter to the Tomb.

The John who was the son of Zebedee was not the writer of the Gospel bearing his name. The scribe who wrote down most of the contents of this Gospel from hearsay accounts and many other sources bore the name John but was not one of the Twelve. He carried out a secretarial duty similar to that undertaken by Polycarp on Patmos, to whom the John who had been Jesus' follower and close companion dictated the memoirs I told you of, that have not yet come to light.

When referring to those who were closest and most faithful to him, Jesus spoke of 'my sons', or on certain occasions 'my brothers' or 'my comrades'. The word 'disciple', which he never used, derives from Greek and Latin, not from the Aramaic. If all those about whom Jesus used those terms had later became known as his disciples, they would have numbered many hundreds.

It is doubtful whether any of the Gospels, with the possible exception of Mark's, were written by one hand. They were compilations based on many sources of information—historical, hearsay, traditional, visionary. There would seem to be no yardstick available to us in modern times by which authorship and identities can be accurately measured in so far as the documents of the New Testament are concerned. There were at least seven Johns closely linked with New Testament narratives; but it would be pointless as well as unwise to attempt to disentangle the many threads coiled round this name.

The Trial and Crucifixion of Jesus

THE GOSPEL ACCOUNTS of the final tragic and momentous events in Jesus' earthly life appear to suggest, or rather to assert, that he was crucified on the morning following his arrest. I am convinced, however, that there is something wrong with the 'time' element in these records. They give the impression of being telescoped into one another in retrospect, in order to 'fit in' with a particular sequence of Jewish rituals and ceremonies associated with the festivals of the season of the Passover.

In fact, the trial of Jesus extended over a considerable period of time, and was a *cause célèbre*, as much political as religious. Everything in Palestine was in a state of uproar. The Romans were obliged to appease the Sanhedrin, without whose co-operation the conquerors would have failed to hold down the subject races. Joseph of Arimathea's post in the Sanhedrin Council precluded him, on legal and technical grounds, from taking any *official* part in the trial, but (as I have told you before) he used his considerable influence in Jewish and Roman quarters *to the full*. For one

81

thing, he provided funds for Jesus to be represented in court by the ablest Jewish advocate of the day; but Jesus refused all help of this kind, and by his own pleadings seemed at times to be almost courting conviction. The prosecution represented him as a dangerous revolutionary —a charge which, although grotesquely exaggerated and distorted, contained *on the face of it* a factual element. But Jesus never attempted to refute this or any of the other charges brought forward by bribed witnesses falsely testifying in an atmosphere blazing with political passions and ferocious religious enmities and intrigues.

In other words, the trial was rigged from the first, and even the semblances of justice were a farcical travesty.

While in prison, Jesus was beaten, scourged, half-starved and isolated. However, he was allowed to see his mother, also his uncle. . . . Jesus' father did not visit him—had not seen him for a year or more. But by then Joseph was sick, semi-paralysed; more or less bed-ridden. Mary Magdalene brought food and fruit. Her love for Jesus was the quintessence of selfless womanly devotion.

Jesus was *destined* to be alone in those final hours upon the Cross, save for the presence of the three Marys and their escort. Witnessing the Crucifixion from as near a point as the soldiers would permit, the Marys formed a Triad whose united courage, faith and love brought solace to Jesus and to those who were crucified with him.

On another level, the presence of the Triad should be seen as an event of truly cosmic significance. Together, these women symbolically foreshadowed the ultimate three-in-one triumphant fusion of the powers inherent in womanly love. They stood before Jesus as a triple promise:

maternal love embodied in his mother Mary; in Mary of Magdala that kind of bond which unites two beings not of the same sex in a love relationship of absolute priority; in the third Mary what might be called love-in-itself; abstract, contemplative.

No doubt about it, the Crucifixion of Jesus was the most inspiring culmination of his life that could have been. By his submission, by his willingness to be lifted up, nailed upon the Cross, that basic symbol of duality, of conflict (it will not be the symbol of the next World Faith), Jesus was 'lifting up' not only humanity but Life in all of the Seven Kingdoms of Nature for the whole of this round of evolution.

But banish from your mind all suggestions of the kind contained in such hymns as, for instance:

> *But the pain which he endured*
> *Our salvation hath assured. . . .*

Thank God, his sufferings upon the Cross were not so unspeakably atrocious. During part of that ordeal when the pain was too great he slipped out of his physical body, and so was freed from intolerable agony. (Even lesser mortals can do this, as I know from experience. On a number of occasions, both in war and peace, while waiting for acute pain to slacken, I have done likewise.) At the same time, he was able, while standing outside his physical form, to relieve the appalling suffering of the two thieves crucified with him.

'My God, My God, why hast thou forsaken me?'
w.t.p.: How to solve the enigma of this supreme Cry which has echoed down the ages; and which, as you say, has provoked—still provokes—more perplexity and scepticism than

any other of Jesus' cryptic recorded utterances: a complex of dilemmas which, so far as I am aware, the Church has said little to alleviate or resolve.

Did Jesus' own faith in his divinity collapse in the final moment? How could it be that Almighty God, Maker of Heaven and Earth, forsook his only begotten Son in the supreme crisis of his earthly life? Such questions have haunted, and continue to haunt, Christians and would-be Christians alike.

The information that follows comes from a source whose wisdom and authority I personally believe to be impeccable. However, it must be clearly understood that my words are not intended to imply final and authoritative pronouncements beyond the reach of error and illusion.

That portion of the immense volume of the Christos Principle which had become individualised within Jesus' aura and in fact which permeated his mind and body, could not, by virtue of its very nature, be subjected to the experience of Crucifixion. Had it remained overshadowing Jesus and within him, as it had for over three years, there could have been no 'death' by Crucifixion, but a miracle of release. (If this sentence appears to embody a contradiction in terms, humanly speaking, I cannot help it!)

Thus, as the final hour approached, the Christos began gradually to withdraw, to renounce its stupendous 'Individualisation' and become merged once more in the Cosmic Principle. It was then that the sense of loneliness (and even failure) overcame Jesus and brought forth that anguished cry of desolation.

You realise, of course, that many readers will find themselves incapable of accepting as truth this interpretation of the supreme enigma of the ages.

As for Josephes, Jesus' cousin and his life-long friend, his absence from Jerusalem at the time of Calvary calls perhaps for explanation.

I cannot speak of this from first-hand knowledge—my information being based on the testimony of hearsay reports current at the time. Josephes was with his wife, the Syrian girl whom he had married the year before, in Arimathea, where he had recently taken over the management of his father's farms. She was expecting his first child, and he considered it his duty to remain with her. News travelled slowly in those days; and although sinister rumours were abroad, definite tidings of Jesus' arrest and trial had not yet reached Judaea. In any case, Josephes knew that his father was in Jerusalem and could be relied on to do everything possible to protect Jesus both from legal action and mob violence.

So soon as his wife was safely delivered, Josephes set out post-haste for Jerusalem, but he arrived too late to be present at the Crucifixion. On the express instructions of his father, he accompanied Mary the mother of Jesus together with the 'beloved disciple' back to Arimathea: a journey fraught with danger from bandits and revolutionaries. Jesus knew that Mary would not desert her husband, and would tend him to his end under the comfortable roof of her new home.

Mary remained in seclusion . . . One of her other children had died—a daughter; also an adopted son. Yes, she was rather lonely, particularly after Joseph of Arimathea was forced to flee from Palestine. But as for the report contained in the Gospel of Nicodemus that he was arrested immediately after the tragedy and remained many years in prison—this is a complete myth. He never lost his freedom, or his freedom of movement.

w.t.p.: In answer to your question what, in Jesus, was most striking and impressive, it would be I think his deep and indestructible serenity. Even one 'standing afar off' in comprehension could see that this serenity was based on an overwhelming certainty: a certainty that embraced the knowledge that Infinite Love and Wisdom ruled the universe; and that nothing, ultimately, could prevail against it. It was as if he gave those around him access to a reservoir of love in which all could bathe with joy and be cleansed, and recover their lost youth.

Then there was a supreme naturalness in all he said and did: a wonderfully illumined simplicity. When he returned from one of his periodic Retreats for meditation, the light streaming from him gave the impression of bodily translucence.

From miles away one could definitely sense the power of his aura. But when he was near, everyone and everything seemed uplifted and irradiated.

It was only when grief or anger invaded him that one became aware of a quality, a majesty, that rendered him unapproachable, remote. Then one was struck with awe. To watch him with children, birds and animals was a revelation of what pure and selfless love can be. At such times all one's own joys and sorrows were dissolved in a sense of ineffable peace: of at-one-ness with the whole of Life and Being. No human words can express the loveliness of such an experience.

At all times, Jesus made one feel a sense of companionship

with him on equal terms. Simplicity, humility, *un*-super-iority: these were the most marked features of Jesus' life, and of all he taught and said and did.

w.t.p.: At the time of the Crucifixion, those around Calvary picked up small chips of wood scattered on the ground, with the idea of preserving them as sacred mementoes; but none of these had formed part of any of the three crosses. This account may come as a shock to those who cherish the belief that relics and fragments of the Central Cross are still extant; but what follows is, I believe, the truth.

When Joseph of Arimathea succeeded in securing the custody of Jesus' body, he also asked for permission to remove the three crosses and hold them for safe keeping. Although Palestine was well-wooded two thousand years ago, timber was a valuable commodity. It was the Roman custom to cleanse, preserve and store such crosses for further use in crucifying criminals; and for this reason, among others, Joseph of Arimathea was determined to obtain possession of the Cross of Calvary and its two companions, even if it meant paying for them in gold: which he did.

He then proceeded to arrange for their transport to the gardens of his Arimathean estate, in Judea. Here they were reverently laid upon the ground, within the olive grove adjoining the estate's farm buildings, where Jesus had spent so many happy days in his boyhood and youth. (The crosses, by the way, were made of mountain oak, and not of olive or cedar wood, as has sometimes been supposed.)

One night, in the course of a solitary meditation on plans for his own future, Joseph of Arimathea received an interior message which he interpreted thus: '*Through cleansing and transformation by fire, your own way forward will be revealed unto you*'. At the time, the problem of what should be done with the crosses, particularly the central one, was one of Joseph's main pre-occupations; and for this reason he linked the message directly with the crosses, and acted accordingly.

On the evening of the following Sabbath day, he summoned his family and his household to the olive grove and asked them to join him in a service of prayer and silence.

This was followed by the removal to higher ground of the three crosses: actually to a clearing within a coppice near the summit of a small hill a few miles distant from the olive grove. Here the crosses were laid, interlaced with one another, on a pyre of reeds, straw and faggots. (This interlacing as a prelude to their reconversion into pristine Energies was ordained for cosmic purposes of great significance.)

Joseph of Arimathea, a learned man with deep reverence for the spirit of Hermes and the ancient lore of sun worship, used his esoteric knowledge in the Prayers of Blessing and of Cleansing; his family meanwhile kneeling around the unlit pyre. Then with his own torch he set fire to the straw and the faggots, and stayed, along with the other witnesses, until all that remained of the crosses was a pile of white ash.

Next morning at sunrise this ash was borne ceremoniously to the highest hilltop on the estate and scattered to the four winds of heaven.

It was in the smoke and flames of that conflagration that Joseph became aware of a stupendous vision. Not only was his own future made manifest, including the great destiny he was to fulfil in the sacred Isle of Britain; but the future of the human race was symbolically revealed to him.

Man and his relations with the Kingdoms of Nature

R.L.: According to w.t.p., Jesus and his comrades are engaged at present on an intensive campaign to further harmonious understanding and co-operation between all forms of life and intelligence throughout all the Seven Kingdoms of Nature known to us and of which we humans are a part; therefore the inclusion of the following Address, w.t.p.'s latest and one of his most important, seems a fitting post-script to the Jesus 'glimpses'. It was originally given to the Companions of the Chalice Well Trust at Glastonbury in 1962; and later published in *Light*. When I first heard it I was struck, as so often, by the parallels between the mind of William Blake and that of w.t.p.

The most practical of English mystics, the most wide-awake and realistic of visionaries, both of them stress the unity of all things; also the quality of life in all things. Blake would have thoroughly understood and appreciated w.t.p.'s conversation with the copper beech tree; and in lines such as these, written nearly two centuries ago, the poet has distilled the essence of his fellow seer's theme.

> *Each grain of Sand,*
> *Every stone in the Land,*
> *Each rock and each hill*
> *Each fountain and rill*
> *Each herb and each tree*
> *Mountain, hill, earth and sea,*
> *Cloud Meteor and Star*
> *Are Men seen Afar.*

w.t.p.: For the first time in recorded history, Man has succeeded in devising a means through which all life on this planet could be extinguished overnight. Ignorant and unwise interference with the rhythm of Nature's laws, mainly through the processes of nuclear fission and their tragic repercussions, could rapidly convert our world into a vast cemetery as the result of atomic warfare, or even accidentally.

For how much longer can we expect the spiritual Powers that be to go on protecting us from ourselves and from those who support the stock-piling of atomic weapons? We may have the power as human beings to destroy ourselves, in a bodily sense, but who gave us the right to endanger the health and the life forces contained within the Kingdoms of Nature.

We are well aware that energy infused with a living intelligence of its own, and in myriad forms, exists and evolves, not only in the mineral, vegetable and animal Kingdoms but in the Kingdoms of Fire, Air and Water as well.

We have come to regard our own species as Lords of Creation, whose dominion over all other forms of life on this planet is not only taken for granted but is considered to be our rightful heritage. In our self-centred egotism, we look upon the denizens of the other Kingdoms as our slaves and therefore expendable solely at our ignorant or wilful discretion.

Is it not time that we began seriously to examine anew our relations with, and our obligations to the life forces in Nature, with which our own evolution and future welfare are so largely allied? Our responsibilities towards all forms of life on this earth are greater than we realise. Can it be said that we recognise this fact and are striving to do our duty by it? To take an example: even if the vivisection of animals can be proved on balance to bring benefits to the human race, are we so sure that such benefits are not being bought at too high a price?

In another field of human action, what right do we possess to subject animals, birds, fish, insects, plants, soil, air, water and trees to the perils of pollution through the widespread release of poisonous radioactivity into their midst?

We appear to have the will to accept such risks for ourselves, mistaken though we undoubtedly are, but why should we think we have the arbitrary right to bring to disaster all other forms of life on this earth which is as much their home as it is ours?

A minority of thoughtful people in the west is beginning to question our right to breed and kill animals, birds and fish to satisfy our appetites. Nature is capable of providing us with ample supplies of nourishment, in the form of grain, cereals, fruit, nuts and vegetables. Is it not foolish therefore, if not actually wrong (a failure to comply with the evolutionary Law) to accept Nature's bounty at second hand rather than direct and at first hand?

The problem of Man's proper relations with the Kingdoms of Nature is too far-reaching to be dealt with adequately on this occasion. My main object in touching upon its fringe is for the purpose of sharing with you a few experiences that have come my way in this connection and which have a direct bearing on the title of these notes. Some of these experiences may appear too trivial to be worth recounting, but seeming trivialities have been known to point the way to truth. For me the experiences now to be related, and many others of a similar kind, have strengthened my conviction that from the standpoint of evolution, life in all its manifestations is indivisible; that is to say, interdependent, whether such life is being expressed in human form or otherwise.

Energy infused with intelligence is by no means confined to the human species. Progression towards higher and more spiritual levels of consciousness must surely be an all-embracing process; one that is certainly not confined to the human race alone.

We will begin with an experience in the African Sahara, now a vast expanse of seeming emptiness; but once green, forest-clad and full of life.

I was sitting on a sand dune alone, watching the sun go down after a day of blinding heat and shimmering mirage. As is often the case in desert regions, a small breeze arose as the sun was setting, stirring the sand around me into gentle eddies. It was then that I became aware of a change of consciousness within myself, accompanied by an alteration in my range of vision. The sand itself gave out a life of its own which seemed to rise up into the breeze and become at one with it. Then it was that I ceased to be a solitary individual, shut away in my bodily form as if in prison.

I found myself communing on equal terms with the spirit of the breeze and with the life of the sand, and I entered into friendly contact with them. All barriers had disappeared and for the time being I was united with the energies of Nature that surrounded me.

Such an experience as this sounds trivial in the telling, but it embraces a reality beyond the power of words to bring to the understanding of other people. Alas! that this should be true of most of the experiences now to be shared with you.

Later, during the same expedition I arrived at a small oasis, already familiar to me from previous visits, I was met by the headman of the tiny community who lived there, and from his bearing realised that something very serious was amiss. The oasis, surrounded by a low wall constructed from briar and primitive bricks of sand, contained a grove of date palms, fig and orange trees, and a carefully tended cereal and vegetable garden. The homes of its forty inhabitants (men, women and children) were single-storeyed and built mainly of similar bricks to those used in the wall around the oasis, which latter kept at bay the ever-encroaching desert sands.

The life of this oasis and its people, together with a few camels, sheep, goats and poultry, depended for its very existence upon a supply of water from a deep well, which at ground level had been extended into an enclosed cistern.

The water from the spring beneath this well was the only source available for drinking, for irrigating the trees and the garden, for the use of the animals, as well as for all household needs.

Never before had this well been known to become dry. Now, however, I was told that the volume of water it contained was diminishing day by day, with the result that the oasis and all it contained might have to be abandoned altogether. This tragic situation was explained whilst I was being escorted to the guest room in the headman's house.

During the evening meal I asked my host to call everyone together to join in prayer that a happy and fruitful solution might be found, in time to avert the need for a general exodus 'into the wilderness'.

They were good Moslems, and therefore received this request with fervour; and we said together a simple prayer to Allah and his Prophet, asking for their grace and succour.

Later I went to my room, sad at the prospect of not being lulled to sleep, as on my previous visits, by the sound of the splash of water in the miniature fountain in the courtyard outside my window.

When I was finally asleep, a change in the rhythm of my consciousness took place, similar to the one already described. My thinking and feeling processes gradually became keyed down or attuned to those of the elemental intelligences in charge of the spring and its surroundings.

I was then able to perceive that at a point about one hundred metres below ground level, a cleavage had opened in the bed of the stream, caused by a 'fault' in the rock strata. As a result the stream, instead of following its customary upward course, was leaking away into the bowels of the earth.

I remember asking the Nature guardians with whom I was then in contact to use our united prayer to help them to repair the leak and so restore the stream to its rightful course. This request was received with every sign of friendliness, but no definite promise was given me.

Very early the next morning, however, I was joyfully awakened by the sound of water bubbling up once more within the little fountain outside my open window.

We then found that the central well was full again; and amidst general rejoicing I went my way. Before doing so, however, I was able to perceive that the leak in the bed of the stream, too far below the surface to be reached by human hands, had been carefully and effectively repaired during the night.

The Affinity of Water with its Parent Source

Whilst on the subject of water, may I refer to another happening somewhat similar to the one I have just described? Throughout the immense and desolate Saudi Arabian desert springs are virtually unknown. At rare intervals along the main camel routes, water-holes are to be found, little more in substance than shallow muddy stagnant pools. From time to time when a caravan arrives at one of these rare drinking places, it is found that the feet of camels or donkeys who had previously passed that way had trampled down the water in the pool to virtual disappearance.

As the next water-hole may be over a hundred miles away, such an occurrence can prove very serious.

I am not familiar with this desert save around its outskirts, and therefore what follows is based on hearsay.

My informant, however, was a man of truth and integrity. He is of Syrian origin and in his time has led many trading caravans across the Arabian deserts on journeys

often lasting for several months at a time. He assured me
that the procedure now to be described is one that he and
other caravan leaders are in the habit of employing when
they find that a particular water-hole en route has become
unusable. I will translate his words: 'On such occasions we
scoop down into the bed of the pool until we come to a
trickle of moisture. This we collect carefully in a goat skin,
even if it may only consist of a few drops. We carry it
with us until we meet a hermit or holy man, to whom we
give the water, telling him the circumstances of the case.
He then calls down the blessing of Allah upon what little
remains of the water we have brought with us, and subsequently sprinkles it upon the ground before him. I have
evidence which for me is beyond dispute that from that
moment onwards, the water-hole in question becomes fully
restored and fit for use again, no matter how distant it may
be.'

One of the strange characteristics of water is that however
far a sample of it is removed from its source, a strong but
invisible link continues to exist between the water in question
and the spring or well from which it was drawn. Wine also
is linked in a similar way with the vineyards from which it
originated.

In recent times, and as the result of experiments in
radiaesthesia, the same living affinity has been found to
exist between a spot of blood and its parent stream, irrespective of the distance between the two.

You may question my object in telling you about such
incidents as these. My aim is to try and make clear the fact
that 'Man does not live unto himself alone'. Under normal
and harmonious conditions there can be maintained close

and friendly relations between us as human beings and the life energies and intelligences in charge of the six other Kingdoms of Nature that are known to us.

Conversation with a Copper Beech

Not long ago, having crossed the Alpine frontier between Austria and Bavaria, I found myself crouching on a narrow plateau just below the snow line.

I had just passed through an exhausting and tragic series of experiences, and as a result was seeking some suitable spot where I could rest awhile. Not far below me, standing on the brink of a precipice, a fine specimen of a copper beech was growing in splendid solitude. Knowing full well the revitalising power these trees possess, I made my way down the mountain side to a point where I was able to wedge myself into a comfortable position beneath the aura and the shelter of this lovely tree.

After a while I was able to become 'keyed' in consciousness to the language of the trees, and I will now try to convert into words the sense of the ideas which passed between me and the spirit of the copper beech.

W.T.P.: What a splendid tree you are, standing here alone! How do you manage to find earth deep enough for your roots to hold you in so tall and upright a position?

C.B.: Thank you, but I am all right because my roots go through concealed crevices in the rock and there is plenty of good earth below . . . You are very kind to ask.

W.T.P.: Wouldn't you like a companion, living as you do so solitary an existence?

C.B.: Yes, sometimes I am lonely. We like to grow up in pairs, but this fact does not seem to be made known to those who plant or seed us.

W.T.P.: Is this desire to live in twos common to all trees, and have trees their own sex?

C.B.: I don't know about other kinds of trees but we much prefer to grow up with a companion, not too close but within 'wind whistling distance'. Some of us feel complete in ourselves, but others need a complementary mate, to make them really happy.

W.T.P.: Thank you very much for telling me this; and now I hope to plant two copper beeches in our Chalice Well Orchard, in England's Glastonbury. But how is one to find out which trees are complementary to one another?

C.B.: You can do this by comparing our young leaves very carefully and then obeying your instinct about them. I have enjoyed our meeting and wish more of your kind could understand us and become our helpmates. Be good to us all and come again.

As I went away stimulated and refreshed, I could not help feeling how wrong and sad it is that we humans have allowed ourselves to become so entirely out of communion with life in the natural worlds around us.

Subsequently; when discussing this experience with an advanced student of metaphysics I was told that oriental tradition associates the copper beech with the planet Mars. According to this tradition Mars was once its native habitat and that since beech seeds found their way to our earth, this particular tree acts as a friendly link between the two planets! To me this is a fascinating idea, however fantastic it may seem to those who think that no relations of any kind exist between the various planets that make up our solar system.

An Experience in the Insect World

There have been accounts in the Press recently telling us of the way in which an English lady has managed to rid her home of beetles, and other unwelcome visitors, by purely peaceful and prayerful means.

I am reminded of a somewhat similar incident which may help to reduce the incredulity with which her experience was received in some quarters.

The summer of 1919 was a particularly sultry one in

Egypt. The flow of the Nile current was so sluggish at the time that the dahabieh on which I was then living became infested with flies and mosquitoes. Neither netting nor disinfectants could keep them at bay, and my guests and myself were unable to eat or sleep without being attacked to a point beyond endurance.

In those days my ability to undertake esoteric experiments was limited, but the situation became so desperate that something had to be done to try to solve the problem. I made the matter a subject of intensive thought and prayer. Within twenty-four hours the answer came. Early in the morning, after rousing myself from disturbed and fitful sleep, I found that a change in the rhythm of my thoughts was taking place, similar to experiences of a parallel kind which have already been described.

Before long I reached a state of consciousness on a level with that apparently possessed by the insect world, and found myself in communion with what can best be described as the elemental spirit within a swarm of mosquitoes which had found its way into my cabin. I explained my predicament and promised that if the mosquitoes could be persuaded to go away and leave us in peace, I would arrange for suitable food to be provided for them each morning on the river bank some distance away from my boat. I confess that at the time I had little hope that this plan would succeed, nor had I much faith in the value of prayer as a sure means for bringing about the end in view.

In any case, although mystified, my cook carried out instructions regularly, and food for mosquitoes was duly provided as promised and at the spot indicated.

Incredible as it may seem, the miracle happened! From

then onwards the mosquitoes (and the flies too!) ceased to plague us either by night or by day. It became possible even to serve meals on open deck without need to use netting or other protective methods.

To this day I look back upon this particular experience with gratitude. In passing, I might mention that on several occasions since, and in various parts of the East, the same means has worked well in flea and beetle infested regions, even without the use of 'bait', through the provision of a meal elsewhere.

There is no good reason why the reader should doubt my accuracy in recounting these experiences even if they are of an unusual kind. He has good right, however, for questioning my interpretation of these incidents, whether they be regarded from a visionary standpoint or from a more concrete level of actuality.

My Friend the Oak Tree

For many years now I have been on friendly terms with a venerable oak tree which is living its long and serene existence at no great distance from my Sussex home.

Recently when I was passing beneath its welcome shade, an

intimation reached me which I was able to interpret in words to the following effect: 'We are unable to prevent what is about to happen to you, but we can safeguard you from any serious consequences. Go forward with care.' At the time and no doubt unwisely, I took little heed of this cryptic warning and continued my stroll, lost in thought that had no relation to possible happenings of a sinister character. Some ten minutes later I found myself suddenly lifted bodily off my feet and hurled into the high bank at the side of the lane along which I was walking. There was no wind at the time, and no other reasonable cause for such a violent occurrence. When I recovered consciousness a minute or two later, I discovered that the bank on which I lay, bruised and breathless, was softly padded with moss and ferns. Had I been flung on to the stony ground of the lane itself, there is no doubt that the consequences would have been serious.

Whilst the physical shock continued for some hours, I was able in due course to get up and return home unaided. The tangible evidence of this experience in the shape of severe and widespread bruises remained to remind me of the incident for many weeks afterwards.

Naturally I sought for a reason to explain such a wanton attack. A week later, whilst passing under my oak tree once more, the following impression reached me. Whether it is a reasonable one I will leave others more conversant with such mysteries to judge.

I had been met by a wandering complex of energy or force which had become detached from its parent complex; perhaps as the result of some atomic disturbance in the ether of the atmosphere. I was used as a kind of lightning conductor to 'earth' safely this dangerous phenomenon. Otherwise, in its uncontrolled meandering, it might well have caused a road accident or even brought about the crashing of an aeroplane. Therefore it was my privilege to give thanks and to go my way rejoicing.

This explanation sounds far-fetched and I do not know who provided it or whether it came from a reliable and authoritative source. If taken at face value, however, one wonders whether some of the many inexplicable accidents that happen so frequently in this hectic age of ours may not be caused by 'wandering and uncontrolled energies that have lost their way'? One thing is certain. There must have been some chink in the armour of my protection to render me vulnerable to such an attack. On analysis, I came to the conclusion that the chink in question had been caused by intense depression at the state of the world as it now is; which depression had been my mental companion for some days before the incident occurred.

It is of course certain that both fear and depression can render one open to 'attack'. What follows will illustrate this fact very aptly.

In the early days of commercial flying, I once made a journey by air from Nice to Lyons. I travelled in a French twin-engined machine and happened to be the only passenger on this particular flight. The heat in Nice had been intense, but so soon as we began to fly over the Alps the cold became intense, no rugs or adequate heating arrangements having been provided.

At this point one of the two motors began to falter, and soon came to a dead stop. My seat was at the front of the plane, from whence I could see the pilot's face through a small window. It soon became evident to me that he had become haggard with fright and was in process of losing his nerve altogether. Let me confess that the sight of his face temporarily destroyed my power to pray or to do more than register fear within myself. It was then borne in upon me very strongly that unless I mastered my own fear and regained my faith and composure, and then transferred these qualities to the pilot, the plane and its living contents would be doomed to disaster.

What follows may make you smile because of its seeming triviality, but this happened to be an occasion when a trivial incident could be used to real advantage. My attention was suddenly distracted by the sight of an ordinary house-fly trying over and over again to climb up the window-pane at my side. It was so engrossed in this task that for some reason I too became momentarily enthralled in watching this by no means unusual incident. Soon I found myself thinking: 'That fly is free from fear and yet I who should know so much better am almost paralysed with dread of what may be about to happen'. Quite illogical reasoning, of course, but curiously effective.

Almost at once all fear left me and I began to send waves of confidence into the mind and the emotions of the pilot, upon whose next actions our lives appeared to depend. It was interesting to watch how the green pallor of his face gradually changed to a more healthy colour and his hands soon ceased to shake. He had succeeded in conquering his fear as I had mine. Being no mechanic, I could not follow the action he then took, but almost immediately the silent motor began to splutter and then to revolve harmoniously once more.

We continued on our way and in due course made a safe landing at Lyons. Subsequently in the bar of the aerodrome lounge the pilot, who was a stranger to me, came over to my corner, shook me warmly by the hand and then said with visible emotion: 'Merci, infiniment, merci pour toujours'.

I have often wondered what he would have said had I told him that he probably owed his life to the presence in the plane of a common house-fly! Undoubtedly it was the infusion of fresh hope and courage at the moment of crisis that had enabled this pilot to take the right decision, which in his intense fear he had been too paralysed to attempt before.

There is a chapter in my book *The Silent Road* in which an account is given of how what might be called a nature spirit has intervened in my affairs, usually to my advantage. I have called this sprightly and always welcome visitor my 'little genie', and although we have never communicated by the use of words, a form of telepathic communion of ideas has proved successful.

When relating these experiences, it has been necessary to convert ideas into actual words, as otherwise such experiences could not be passed on intelligibly to those who are unfamiliar with the processes of wordless telepathy. As a result, and quite naturally, some of my correspondents have expressed their incredulity in no uncertain terms. This fact underlines the difficulties involved in sharing 'other-worldly' happenings with those to whom such a field of research is unfamiliar. In passing let me say how convinced I am of the existence of what the Irish call the 'Little People', that is, nature spirits, fire and water elementals and other non-human forms of being in immense variety, living out their useful lives in and around our human world, invisible to most of us yet as real and living as we ourselves.

There is one problem which seems to be almost insoluble in this respect. It is never easy to separate, even in one's own mind, what might be called a visionary experience from an external incident, which latter may or may not follow the experience in question.

An experience taking place within the mind can prove both real and actual to the visionary himself, irrespective of whether it is accompanied by any kind of external manifestation. When one tries, for instance, to pass on to others a description of such happenings as these notes contain, one finds it almost impossible to define even to oneself the exact point at which an interior vision or experience merges into an external event. I have not yet succeeded in finding a way by which this difficulty can be overcome.

Who among us is capable under all circumstances of making a clear distinction between that which is 'real' and that which is the figment of a lively and illusory imagination?

I remember an occasion when my little genie, arriving unexpectedly out of the blue, as is his usual custom, asked me why many humans behaved so strangely as they went about their daily lives. When I asked him what he meant, he replied in ideas which could be translated into the following words:

'They nearly always seem to be chasing shadows which they believe to be realities. On the other hand they ignore altogether what are realities to us and therefore much more interesting and valuable.'

It is disconcerting to think that there may be truth in this remark. Are we not very much addicted to 'chasing shadows' whilst ignoring the substance from which these shadows are derived?

I hope that by now the main reason for sharing some of my experiences has become clear. I have been trying to show that no rigid barriers need separate us humans from other varieties of life and intelligence that have their being in the six Kingdoms of Nature; we ourselves belonging to the seventh.

The progressive evolution of life throughout these seven Kingdoms moves forward as a whole and not separately. Life is a unity and all its manifestations in form, both visible and invisible, are interdependent upon one another. It is for this reason that we should begin to understand and practise this truth and conscientiously accept the responsibilities that flow from it.

A Conversation

R.L.: IN THE BELIEF that the matters touched upon in the course of this conversation, which took place one afternoon in November 1963, will be of interest and value to many besides myself, I have asked W.T.P.'s permission to reproduce a portion of it.

R.L.: I can't bring myself to say 'pass on', 'pass over'—all those terms spiritualists use when speaking of death. They sound so euphemistic and genteel. But I notice that you too always speak of someone's 'passing' when you mean his or her death. What is the point of avoiding this blunt time-honoured word? To take the sting out of it?
W.T.P.: There are more effective means of taking the sting out of it! . . . But there are Powers and Principalities dedicated to bringing about the total disappearance of individual life as we humanly understand it. They work for the dissolution of the human soul's individuality in the eternal ocean of Life Unmanifest: to precede an entirely

new era of evolution in fresh patterns. To this end, these Powers co-operate with man's persistent efforts to destroy himself by nuclear explosion, and other forms of the misuse of his free will.

They are unlikely to succeed.

But whenever we use the word 'Death' in relation to Life, or to the continuity of each individual entity, we provide ammunition for these Powers. We are sowing the wrong mental seeds with results potentially most disastrous . . . Actually it's incorrect to speak even of the 'death' of the physical body, because it dissolves into a thousand energies and emanations, even if cremated . . . to say nothing of the central core, which is transmuted and absorbed into the soul's mental form or body. Sooner or later this core forms the crux—or foundation—for the same soul's next incarnating physical form. This is the resurrection of the body, properly understood.

(When I reported this information to a dear friend, c.s., who, by virtue of years of discipline and dedication, has trained herself to become a miraculously pure clairaudient channel for communication, she said: 'Perhaps that's why I always feel guilty when I use that word'. But we agreed that the alternatives are unsatisfactory; and that, possibly, exceptions might be made for such triumphant challenges as Browning's *Prospice*; or Donne's great poem beginning: '*Death, be not Proud . . .*', and that in any case to use the word as it were in 'quotes', and with understanding, must surely exonerate us.

R.L.: About the soul body: could you tell me something more?

W.T.P.: Just as the etheric counterpart of the physical is the link with the next form in which we manifest after death, the soul body is the counterpart or vehicle of the mind. Just as the navel cord links the infant physically with its mother, each higher vehicle has a luminous or 'silver' connecting channel: formed firstly of etheric substance; secondly of soul substance.

The etheric shroud can be full of discordant elements. When it dissipates, and the emergent being is really functioning in his new body, the whole substance of this shroud becomes precipitated. That is what creates the almost concrete layer which surrounds human consciousness . . . surrounds the etheric counterpart of the planet itself.

R.L.: I've read and heard so much about reincarnation in the last few years. I believe in it, of course——.

W.T.P.: Oh, you do! . . . I gather it's becoming quite a respectable topic, even in ecclesiastical circles.

R.L.: But so many of the pronouncements and theories—from 'the other side' as well as this—seem to be contradictory.

W.T.P.: It's an immense subject; and a very subtle one. A good deal of the confusion arises because it isn't understood that very few of those now on earth are here in full incarnation.

R.L.: You mean, most of one's self, or a large proportion of it, lives so to speak 'over there'?

W.T.P.: That is part of what I mean. The Ego sends down different Rays from itself, one at a time, to learn discipline and gain experience. That is why memories of past lives on earth are so very difficult to define or to recollect. Ultimately, the Ego re-absorbs all its Rays; and then, when its human evolution on this planet is nearing completion, sends down into incarnation its completed soul as a single entity.

But at least thirty per cent, probably more, of human beings now on earth are not yet really individualised; they are still portions of group souls.

R.L.: Is there any fixed law governing the number of incarnations on this planet?

W.T.P.: No, there is no fixed law; and the number varies largely in accordance with each Ego's status and development *before* the present twenty-five thousand year Round of Evolution began.

Most people hate the idea that their total individual entity does not incarnate until many separate sections of it have experienced a series of earth lives. And of course there is a danger of feeling complete in a material sense: one tends to cut oneself off from invaluable contact and communion with one's Mother Soul.

Anyone who has started seriously on the path of selfless service can call down from his or her own Ego whichever particular Rays are needed for the work in hand.

Of course, what I am telling you only touches the fringe of the subject.

R.L.: How can the Christ or Christos be defined?

W.T.P.: The Cosmic Christ Universal is a Divine Principle, not a 'person'. It is a Quality, an Emanation from the Godhead. It is true that when this Christ Principle over-shadows an Initiate or a Master—or indeed a lesser mortal—the experiences, the sensations, the intelligence of these chosen channels are permanently heightened and extended;

but the Principle Itself does not undergo evolutionary or other changes. It cannot suffer, for instance; or in any other way be subject to the human situation. Eternally, It IS. But before the Christ can descend further into human life in all its aspects—before a new age can dawn—It has to have the co-operation of mankind. . . . You can think of It as awaiting our response, our full co-operation now.

R.L.: How can the Logos be defined?

W.T.P.: The Logos is simply and solely the Word, the Creative Word through which rhythm was generated as the basis for the manifestation of life in all its forms. Not a Quality or an Emanation.

The Christos is under the direction of the Divinity that controls the entire solar system of planets, stars and satellites.

The Master or Ruler of this planet (who is an Individual) is responsible for sending out into manifestation Messengers representing Himself. He calls upon the Solar God to grant Him the services of the Christos: He is the Channel through which the Christos overshadows the Messengers.

R.L.: What are the attributes of the Ruler of this planet? Can He be described?

W.T.P.: He has the direction of all life upon this earth, His planet. He is the dispenser of all the qualities we sum up as Love, Light, Wisdom. You can talk of Him in human terms. You can commune with Him.

R.L.: Do you pray to Him?

W.T.P.: I address my prayers through Him to the Principle of all Life throughout the Universe. But if it be a matter directly affecting the planetary Ruler—such as acting as a herald, or carrying out a quest—then I commune with Him —because it's His affair.

R.L.: In *The Silent Road* you speak with disapproval, if not condemnation, of trance mediumship, 'automatic' writing, circles—all that. This has caused anxiety to some of your readers who long to get in touch with their 'dead' and fear from what you say that they should not seek such sources of consolation in bereavement; or attempt to develop their own psychic faculties. I felt you were too sweeping in your strictures.

W.T.P.: It may be that I was. But I have had to deal with so much human wreckage resulting from people's ignorant or excessive self-exposure to physical phenomena. . . . What we've got to understand is that those who have gone on are subject, at first at least, to far more fluidic and illusory conditions than we are. They aren't by any means always able to free themselves from the two-way pull of gravitation, terrestrial versus spiritual. In the so-called Plane of Illusion, where many of us linger, you can mould the atmosphere into any form you like by manipulating its magnetic energies and currents. Trance mediums also utilise these currents: you can see the danger: they may open doorways—two-way doorways—to delusion, confusion—even to serious obsessional influences. The results may prove far more injurious than we realise; not to speak of the danger of detriment to the health—mental and physical—of those who go in for trance methods.

R.L.: I accept what you say: I understand. But I still think such an authority as yourself should, could, help people more positively in this field . . . help them to discriminate, distinguish for themselves. Why must the watchwords always be 'Beware!' 'Avoid!' 'Mistrust!'? It seems to me that 'break-throughs' are starting everywhere: ordinary people like myself—not just the elect or the select—are having genuine extra-sensory experiences. Warnings are all very well, but what we really need is enlightened encouragement.

w.t.p.: Do you, indeed! Surely you don't imagine I can provide *that*? . . . However, I'd like to explain as clearly as I can—I'd like to emphasise—that the human race is now entering a new dispensation. Fresh spiritual perceptions, new agencies for communion between different levels of consciousness will develop: will bring about a gradual spiritual-gravitational upward pull to get us off the ground . . . away from where we are now: grounded!

Also I would like to say that it is far from my intention to question the sincerity and the dedicated service to humanity of numerous fine mediums past and present. You know and admire some personally, and so do I; and in any case the abandoning of trance methods must be gradual. But on the whole I would say that now is the time for all true seekers to relinquish trance mediumship, automatism, materialisation circles and the rest. These forms of psychic phenomena and investigation belong to the period of the downward arc. Remember we are at the very lowest point of this round of evolution—waiting for the impulse to generate the upward urge. We have an urgent duty to bring about less tension in the worlds into which we pass at death. We must try to lift ourselves in consciousness to a point where contact—communion—can take place on a plane above the pull of terrestrial gravitation—free of it. Our destiny is to ascend, you know: to 'die' less and less. We mustn't hang on to anything that makes for further descent into matter—for more 'death'.

However, don't go putting self-evolution in its wrong place. What does your rating or percentage matter? All that matters is to do your job of preparation.

R.L.: What should be the 'job' of mediums nowadays? How should they prepare themselves?

W.T.P.: Well . . . I would say, I think, to a trance medium: 'If you wish to use your gifts in connection with the New Age, pray before going into trance, pray that the entity whom you trust, who is going to take possession of your organism, points the way to the methods of the New Age. Help people to understand what the stilling of self means; what the prayer of selfless receptivity means; how to begin to rise towards a level on which we can commune with those we love without an intermediary.

(R.L.: Recently I came across a remarkable letter from the poet Rilke, written originally to my friend the late Countess Nora Wydenbruck, in answer to a letter recounting certain psychical experiences of hers. Certain passages seem so relevant that I cannot forbear to quote them—as a theme for meditation.

RILKE: 'I am convinced that these phenomena, if we accept them without making them a means of escape and remain willing to co-ordinate them with the whole of our existence . . . I am convinced that these phenomena do not merely satisfy a false curiosity but concern us indescribably. . . . If the dead, and those who are still to come, should need a dwelling place, what refuge could be more fitted to their needs than these mansions of the mind? To me it appears like this: our ordinary consciousness dwells on the apex of a pyramid, whose base within us stretches out so far that, the deeper we penetrate into it, the more we find ourselves at one with the events of earthly life, in the widest sense of cosmic life, which are independent of time and space. . . . Now these seances, with all their disturbing or misleading side-issues, their clumsiness, their half-truths and (there can be no doubt) their countless misunderstandings, lie on the road to such knowledge(i.e. that past, present and future are different modes of the eternal Now). They could not surprise me. . . . I should have felt something was missing if I had not known such things to happen! But just because my inner beliefs have always accepted the miraculous as natural I refused to devote myself to these revelations rather than to any other mystery of life; to me they are one secret more among innumerable secrets. . . . But while I accept them humbly, seriously, and reverently, my instinct leads me to awaken something in my consciousness to counterbalance them as soon as they have penetrated it; nothing could be more alien to my nature than a world where these phenomena had the upper hand. . . . What do we know of the seasons of eternity and whether it happens to be harvest time? How many fruits which were meant for us, or whose weight alone could have caused them to fall at our feet—how many fruits such as these have been checked in their ripening by inquisitive minds, who could win nothing but a hasty premature understanding, often a misunderstanding, at the price of the uplifting and nourishment that was not ready, and that they thus destroyed?')

R.L.: To go back for a moment to the magnetic pulls and currents you spoke of: do they account, for instance, for the sense of depression, of motiveless apprehension I get in thundery weather?—or before any violent change in the weather? I mean, does the electric disturbance occur primarily in the inner planes?—at a more psychic level of pressure, so to speak?

W.T.P.: There is no event that takes place in the three-dimensional world which hasn't already taken place in the four-dimensional world.

R.L.: What is the difference between psychic and spiritual vision?

W.T.P.: Psychic vision is simply extended physical sight. It operates through the senses. You might call it a linking or three-and-a-half dimensional vision. The psychic seer is half in and half out of time-space conditions.

Spiritual vision is the vision of the mind, which can be used on any plane, and is therefore completely free from the intrusion of the senses; and therefore clearer and more accurate than psychic vision.

By the way, there's no such thing, in reality, as the 'etheric plane' or the 'astral plane'. These terms represent (and sometimes misrepresent) states or degrees of consciousness. The 'realm' of the etheric can be purgatorial. Then you go one step higher, into the mental realm: which is where certain Beings well known to me have their habitation and perform their manifold tasks and duties, and entertain their friends even while still functioning on earth in physical bodies. This realm is divided into two. The upper mental is where all desires, even on behalf of others, all self-centred urges are to be shed. The extent to which one is capable of shedding determines the extent to which one can become fully awake or conscious in 'Paradise'. You can see for yourself what a difference that makes!—to be able to be consciously in touch with your Guide . . . to confer with him . . . to be no longer only half awake.

R.L.: Does everyone have a Guide?

W.T.P.: No. Once an Ego is fully integrated, then a personal guide becomes available. But as I've told you already, only a small proportion of people now incarnate are individualised.

R.L.: Why is the 'astral plane' so called?

W.T.P.: The reason for the use of the word 'astral' is that the luminosity in this condition we shall wake up in after death appears to be 'starry' rather than 'sunny'. The degree of luminosity, so far as the individual is concerned, depends upon the extent to which he or she can be a pure reflector or radiator of that luminosity. In other words, although this starry light appears to be outside you, it is also within you. If you enter that plane 'dark', 'in darkness', you carry the dark within you and cannot reflect the light. So you remain in semi-obscurity or dense twilight.

Progress while passing through 'astral conditions' depends almost entirely on the extent to which you can cleanse the mirror of your consciousness to reflect the starry radiation: which in itself is a reflection once removed of the Christ Light. Pure Christ Light cannot be seen; but when transmitted thus it can be both seen and measured.

Certain Initiates and Adepts make a point of descending into the dark regions of Borderland in order to leave behind them a trail of light. I have often watched this. . . . Even from earth levels one can watch the trail of light that one of these great Beings leaves behind him. Each of us as we purify our consciousness begins to radiate and diffuse this light.

R.L.: I was reminded of a description that my daughter Sally gave me, through a channel I have learnt to trust, of her second Christmas 'over there'. She said: 'The Shining Ones come down and scatter . . . scatter radiance . . . wisdom'. Another time she referred to 'The Brighter Ones'.

R.L.: Gurdjieff taught that one must gain one's immortal soul during one's life on earth. Otherwise one is threatened— to use his sinister phrase—with being 'candidate for perishing like a dog'. Is this true doctrine?

W.T.P.: No. Wrong usage. Your immortal soul is given to you: you don't gain it. The discipline of earth life is immensely important; but you can become an integrated being on any of the spheres at any level of consciousness. Blavatsky also tends to perpetuate this very ancient concept: namely that progress, that is evolution, can only take place on earth levels. Nothing could be further from the truth. No one ever stands still. We are not ushered right away into a realm of eternal bliss; nor are we consigned to purgatorial negation. In cases of great degradation of a human being, a transmigration from one level to another, lower, *can* occur. There may be a merging into the animal—or the vegetable—or even the mineral world; but this is for the express purpose of learning some lesson that we missed learning before, and which can only be taught us at a lower level of comprehension and rhythm. There is no death. . . .

This law of merging operates of course in the other, higher direction. It can apply even to the Ruler of this Planet. By an act of free will, by giving himself up as a sacrifice, he can be absorbed into the Principle of All Life.

R.L.: Could you explain more about the Akashic Records?

W.T.P.: Every thought, emotion and action throughout all the Kingdoms of Nature creates a vibration in the spiritual etheric substance. Each of these vibrations is photographed or imprinted in such a way that it is indelible. The negatives, so to speak, are all available: if you know how, you can make the prints! The whole story has been implanted in the spiritual etheric substance and cannot be effaced.

Each one of us has his or her own Akashic record as soon as our souls become individualised. We can relate our personal record to the whole planetary record. We can observe how we've advanced it . . . or damaged it.

R.L.: Could you enlighten me about the correct use of such terms as 'Adept', 'Initiate', 'Master'? I know you are chary of them.

W.T.P.: There are seven gateways of Initiation: that is, seven levels of enlightenment available to the human spirit. Let us suppose one has gone through the first gateway: before one comes to the second there are seven subsidiary steps to be taken.

One is permitted the use of the term 'Adept' when one has reached the entrance to the second gateway. An Adept is one who has reached a clear perception of the laws of Nature.

By the time one reaches the seventh step before the third gateway one will have gained a clear perception of the spiritual counterparts of the laws of Nature. One is now a high grade Adept.

Once through the third gateway, and up to the seventh step before the fourth, one is an Initiate. One is given the perception of the relations between the Creator and the Created.

When one has gone through the fourth gateway one becomes an Initiate of the first degree; and one is given the perception of the laws governing the whole of the Cosmos.

Past the fifth gateway, one is a Master in the natural worlds of this and other planets; past the sixth, a Master in the supernatural worlds.

When one is through the seventh gateway, one is given the Keys of the Universe! One is beyond the Master level: one belongs to the Christ degree and can impregnate the Masters with one's luminosity.

You shouldn't—you can't—measure the stature of one Master against another. Each is an individualised expression of the Godhead, standing at a different point within the orbit of perfection.

Shall I tell you something else? A great many of the holy men and spiritual leaders on our planet are through the first gateway, but no further.

And here's a piece of knowledge to give any of us pause: if you have started on the Path, and you turn back, then you are really for it. It's not an unmixed blessing to possess psychic or occult gifts: they can generate a false sense of security . . . Spiritual pride masquerading as humility is a very unpleasant sight. All too common. . . .

R.L.: Do Initiates inevitably recognise one another?

W.T.P.: Yes. Each carries a 'lamp'. Its particular kind of

light discloses the bearer's spiritual stance.

This Path is the one on which one renders the greatest service to one's fellow men. But there are many many individual souls who are destined to evolve in quite a different way. . . . The routes are myriad, and lead to the same goal.

W.T.P.: I get the impression that a whiff of dogmatism appears to have found its way into some of my replies to your questions. Do make it clear that any awareness of truth I may possess is by no means final in its certitude. Truth has a million million facets and absolute truth is beyond our human comprehension.

All other forms of truth are relative, and as much subject to the evolutionary process as our understanding of them. No reader should accept anything that offends his reason or his understanding at the point at which he now stands.

One Word More

W.T.P.: We were a patrician family with Assyrian roots —non-Hebrew—and we continued to revere the Gods in the pure uncontaminated Greek sense. We were not very sympathetic towards the various contesting sects whose adherents milled around Jesus and the early Nazarenes. One supreme Creator above all the Gods: yes; but a broad universality of outlook, as rare in Christian times as it is today: that was the mental background against which I looked upon Jesus, seeing him as a Man of the Gods, and a great Seer. (In *The Upper Room* I think I refer to crossing

the city on my way back to my own home.) We also had
estates in Syria and a house near Aleppo. My only brother
was an authority on precious stones and metals. He it was
who first introduced me to Joseph of Arimathea—who in
any case was a friend of my father's and of the family.

Much to my mother's grief I never married; and later in
life became much withdrawn, working *au delà* as well as
upon the earth; as I do today.

R.L.: Perhaps a voiceless voice, nearest and dearest in all
the worlds known to me, may be permitted one word more,
by way of adding her signature to this task which I have
attempted; and which, but for her absence and her presence,
would never have been undertaken.

SALLY: Yes, I have seen and heard and met him in the
inner planes during sleep. Yes, he has had many lives before,
and has known the Mysteries and used them, forgotten
and re-discovered them. His spirit goes out and out, and his
mission is veiled from me. Perhaps it will only receive real
fruition over here.

There is a light in the spirit of man illuminating everything, and by which he may even perceive supernatural
things. Those who seek in the light of external Nature know
the things of Nature; those who seek knowledge in the light
of man know the things above Nature, which belong to the
kingdom of God. Man is an animal, a spirit, and an angel,
for he has all three qualities. As long as he remains in Nature
he serves Nature; if he moves in the spirit, he serves the
spirit (in him); if he lives in the angel, he serves as an angel.
The first quality belongs to the body, the two others to the

soul, and they are its jewels. The body of man remains on earth, but man, having a soul and the two additional qualities, is enabled to rise above Nature, and to know that which does not belong to Nature. He has the power to learn all that belongs to heaven and hell, to know God and His kingdom, the angels and the spirits.

—PARACELSUS

Epilogue

In recent years a curious spate of 'authoritative' pronouncements on the subject of Jesus, his crucifixion and resurrection has surfaced in various quarters. It is alleged, for instance, that his disciples removed him, still breathing, from the Cross, secreted him for a while until, his health restored, he slipped away to India, where he died at a ripe old age. Then, in a recent best-seller, we are given a dramatic account purporting to be researched in depth and historically proven. Distinguished scholars, historians, emphatically dispute this latter claim. No matter, says the public. Are not scholars always blinkered? In any case it is a thrilling, a fascinating work of detection, replete with cryptic clues; and with the compulsive appeal of a good detective thriller.

There is also a huge American paperback publication entitled *Seth Speaks*. Through his entranced medium Jane Roberts, 'Seth', allegedly an advanced discarnate being, has communicated a wealth of philosophical and scientific material, much of it of genuine interest and importance.

But when he comes to speak of Jesus and the Crucifixion, he descends (to my mind) to a level so vulgar, bogus, specious, as to be totally unacceptable, not to say repellent. The testimony of the four gospels is summarily dismissed. The symbolism underlying the greatest and most ancient of all cosmic dramas is set at nought with breezy self-assurance. I quote: *'Jesus had no intention of dying in this manner....'* *'That wasn't his game....'* *'There was a conspiracy in which Judas played a role, an attempt to make a martyr out of Christ....'* *'The man chosen was drugged, (hence the necessity of helping him carry his cross) told that he was Christ and believed it....'* *'The reason for Peter's three-fold denial was quite simple: he knew that the man chosen to be crucified wasn't Jesus....'* *'He (Jesus) was a clever magician – he appeared in various post-mortem guises, even managing to produce a simulacrum of his wounds....'* And so on, and so on *ad nauseam.*

Not long before his departure in 1968 I showed these passages to W. T. P. The result was elecrifying: he was seized with a fierce transpersonal rage. 'As if,' he blazed, 'a wonderful chap like Jesus, the soul of integrity, integrity incarnate, could conceivably stoop to such a dirty trick – could permit a wretched innocent man to be drugged, deluded, sent in his place to die in agony.'

From time to time I am still enabled to get in touch with W. T. P. through the pen of Cynthia Sandys (see also *The Awakening Letters*). A few months ago, she and I were discussing these so-called 'novel and challenging viewpoints.' Did they really matter? We thought that they did. It was as if we were being told that Christianity is an outworn myth, meaningless in these enlightened days.

Suffering is out of fashion, death can be deprived of its spiritual significance, discreetly removed from all distressing images and associations. I spoke of W. T. P. and wondered what fresh insights he might have achieved from *au delà*. 'Let us ask him,' said Cynthia. He seemed to us both to have drawn very near. After a silence she took up her pen and wrote what follows with extreme rapidity and power.

W. T. P.: November 1982. My dear Alexias, So you are wondering what happened to Jesus two thousand years ago. Well – as I told you, he *was* crucified – the *man* was: but you cannot crucify the spirit (as you were saying a few minutes ago).* But this having happened in the most horrible and brutal way, the Lords of Karma decided that mankind had not grown sufficient intelligence to understand the body and spirit as separate beings. The crowd were entirely taken in by what they could see and grasp. When the spirit evaded them, they were absolutely at sea and didn't know what to think.

The body of Jesus having been impregnated by the vibrations of the Christ was not completely mortal, so could not 'die'. When the feeling of desertion on the Cross had left him, he allowed the Christ vibration to gather momentum. . . . And after a certain time he became alive in the tomb, and able to remove the grave clothes and free himself as spirit. This was due to the Christ within and without bearing upon the physical body and causing it to vanish – as all things physical do when under Christ power.

* *In conversation with C. S.*

129

But he realised the great loss and misery his fate was causing to his human mother; and so for a time, on several occasions he assumed a body, telling them not to touch him, but making his appearances plain. Now this was a manifestation of the complete integration of spirit, mind and body. They were made whole for a time. But even so, the disciples did not recognise this composite body. It was only during the breaking of bread that the spirit withdrew a little, and the physical came to the fore.

I know this is a difficult 'passage of thought' between the spirit and the body which appeared again and again, even allowing doubting Thomas to touch the nail scars and the spear thrust. But Jesus and the Christ became completely mingled into one personality: so that Jesus can be – and is – worshipped as the Christ. It was a marvellous ritual of Mind, Body and Spirit, and one to dwell upon and meditate upon endlessly.

Don't worry about the Churches if they attack you. Go with them. If they don't accept you let them go. We have the real Christ here; so we can laugh and dream and exclaim and wonder at the intense virility of this plan.

★   ★   ★

I am grateful to Neville Armstrong of Neville Spearman for agreeing to let me include this Epilogue in his paperback reprint of *A Man Seen Afar*.

Rosamond Lehmann.   April 1983.